R

Paul I.

George I.

Yukon R.

Kuskokwim R.

RUSSIAN

Yukon R.

L. Iliamna

KENAI PEN.

Chugach Bay

Mt.
St. Elias•

AMERICA

ALASKA PEN.

Kenai Bay

Nuchek I.
Montague I.

Resurrection Bay

Yakutat Bay

Yakutat

Pavlovsk Harbor
(Kodiak)

Kodiak I.

Sitka
(Novo-Arkhangel'sk)

OCEAN

BARANOV

CHIEF MANAGER OF THE RUSSIAN COLONIES IN AMERICA

By

K. T. KHLEBNIKOV

Translated by
COLIN BEARNE

Edited by
RICHARD A. PIERCE

THE LIMESTONE PRESS
BOX 1604
KINGSTON, ONTARIO K7L 5C8

BARANOV

CHIEF MANAGER OF THE RUSSIAN COLONIES IN AMERICA

International Standard Book Number 0-919642-50-0

Printed and bound in Canada by: Brown & Martin, Limited
Kingston, Ontario

This is number *143* of a first printing of *530* copies.

Contents

Baranov's journey to Yakutat,
building of fort. News of the
party. <u>1797</u>: Baranov's travels
to Kenai and Chugatsk Bays.
Occupation of these places.
Arrival of vessel [<u>Phoenix</u>,
Talin] from Okhotsk. News of
Shelikhov's death. <u>1798</u>:
Departure of the Archimandrite
for Irkutsk [on <u>Phoenix</u>, Shields].
Baranov's journey along the North-
west Coast of America.   12

Baranov's journey thence and his
return. Arrival of American ship
[O'Cain, O'Cain]. Agreement with
the Captain on sea otter hunting.
Success and return to Kad'iak.
1804: Navigator Bubnov [arrives
on baidarka from Unalashka].

Chapter V: Sending of vessels [Ekaterina
and Aleksandr] to Yakutat, and
from there to Sitka. Mishap in
Icy Strait. Arrival in Sitka.
The Neva [Lisianskii]. Warlike
activities. Taking of the fort.
Dispatch of Neva to Kad'iak.
Dispatch of party from Sitka for
hunting, and to Kad'iak. 1805:
Return of Neva from Kad'iak and
departure to Canton. Arrival of
brig Elisaveta [Sukin] from
Okhotsk, then of brig Maria
[Mashin] with the Company representative Rezanov. His
instructions on the founding of
the colonies. Purchase of ship
Juno [from D'Wolf]. Award of
medal. Departure of Juno for
Kad'iak and return from there
with supplies.

Chapter VI: News of the wreck of the
Elisaveta [Sukin] and other misfortunes. Description of the
disaster suffered by Dem'ianenkov's party. Destruction of the
fort at Yakutat, and Kolosh intentions to destroy the settlement at Nuchek. 1806: Departure of Juno [Khvostov] for
California and the securing of
grain from there. Departure of
Rezanov [on Juno, Khvostov] for
Okhotsk. Remarks on Khvostov's
Japanese expedition [with Juno,
and Avos']. Agreement with
Capt. Winship [O'Cain] on sea
otter hunting, and its results.
Present from the Sandwich Island
King Kamehameha. Agreement with
skipper O'Cain [Eclipse] about
delivery of goods to Nagasaki
and Canton. Departure thence of
the ship Eclipse. Trading in
Canton, adventures in Japan on
return journey. Visit to Kamchatka. Wreck of the Eclipse

off Sannakh Island. The vessel
rebuilt; its loss and the death
of O'Cain.

ILLUSTRATIONS

A. A. Baranov (drawing by Tikhanov, 1818)

G. I. Shelikhov (from Tikhmenev)

N. P. Rezanov (from Tikhmenev)

I. A. Kuskov (from portrait made at Fort Ross in 1813, in Tot'ma Regional Studies Museum, U.S.S.R.)

Three Saints Bay, Kodiak Island, 1790 (from S.G. Fedorova, <u>Russkoe naselenie Aliaski i Kalifornii</u>, M., 1971)

Pavlovsk Harbor, Kad'iak, 1798 (from A. V. Efimov, <u>Atlas geograficheskikh otkrytii</u>..., M., 1964)

Novo-Arkhangel'sk (Sitka), 1805 (from Lisianskii)

Fort Ross in 1817 (from S. G. Fedorova, <u>Russkoe naselenie Aliaski i Kalifornii</u>, M., 1971)

Maps, end papers:

    Russian America under Baranov

    Kad'iak Island, 1805 (from Lisianskii)

    The Northwest Coast, from Yakutat Bay to Sea Otter Bay, about 1813 (from Lisianskii)

INTRODUCTION

Kiril Timofeevich Khlebnikov, whose life of Baranov is published here in English translation for the first time, might himself be the subject of a biography. He was born in the town of Kungur, on the western slope of the Ural Mountains, in 1776. In 1800 he entered the employ of the newly-formed Russian-American Company and served first in the Company headquarters in Irkutsk, and then, in 1801, as the Company prikashchik or agent in Kamchatka. There he spent the next twelve years, often in privation, and sometimes at great personal risk, closely involved in Russia's ventures in the North Pacific. In 1805, he met the round-the-world ship Nadezhda, under Captain Krusenstern, bearing the pleni-potentiary N. P. Rezanov from his unsuccessful mission to Japan. In the winter of 1806 and 1807, he traversed Kamchatka with the naturalist G. H. von Langsdorf, just returned from Russian America, and then sailed to Okhotsk with him on the small sailboat Rostislav, commanded by Captain John D'Wolf. In November, 1811, he was one of the first on the scene of the wreck of the Company ship Juno, on the coast of Kamchatka.

In 1813, his health undermined by years of hardship, Khlebnikov left for Irkutsk and St. Petersburg. At the capital he accepted the post of office manager for the Company headquarters in America, to be part of a re-organized colonial administration to follow the retire-ment of the aged A. A. Baranov. In September, 1816, he started around the world as supercargo on the Kutuzov, under Captain Hagemeister, and arrived at Novo-Arkhangel'sk (Sitka) on November 20, 1817. There he aided A. A. Baranov, retiring chief manager, in the

final totting up of accounts, gaining a first hand
acquaintance which later aided his biography. For the
next sixteen years Khlebnikov served under Baranov's
successors--Ianovskii, Murav'ev, Chistiakov, and Baron
Wrangell. He trained employees for all branches of
Company administration, dealt fairly with the natives,
and several times sailed to California, Mexico, Peru
and Chile on Company business. In his spare time he
learned Spanish and English, studied the natural history
of Russian America, read widely, and augmented his
knowledge of the region by talks with seafarers,
visiting scientists, and Company officials.

In 1832, exhausted by thirty years of service, and
with sufficient means saved up to provide security in
his old age, he left Sitka for Russia. He sailed on the
war sloop Amerika on November 30, 1832, and arrived at
Kronshtadt on September 13, in the following year. Because of his experience, honesty, and ability, the
Company appointed him Manager of Affairs, and in 1835 he
was elected to serve on the Board of Directors. He was
awarded the Order of St. Anna, 3rd Class, and was made a
corresponding member of the St. Petersburg Academy of
Sciences. This culmination of his career was to be
short, however; he died on April 15, 1838.

Khlebnikov's writings are a valuable source of
information about the Russian-American Company colonies.
The six part manuscript "Zapiski o koloniiakh v Amerike
Rossiisko-Amerikanskoi kompanii" (Notes on the Russian-
American Company's colonies in America), in the Archive
of the Geographical Society of the USSR, contains many
facts and statistics unavailable elsewhere. Two of the
six parts, on Sitka and Fort Ross, were published in
1861 in a supplement to the periodical Morskoi sbornik
[Naval Symposium] in Materialy dlia istorii russkikh
zaselenii po beregam vostochnago okeana [Materials for
the history of the Russian settlements on the shores of
the Eastern Ocean]. See R. G. Liapunova, "Rukopis K. T.

Khlebnikova 'Zapiski o koloniiakh v Amerike' kak
istochnik po etnografii i istorii Aliaski i Aleutskikh
ostrovov," [K. T. Khlebnikov's manuscript 'Notes on the
colonies in America' as a source for the ethnography
and history of Alaska and the Aleutian Islands] in Ot
Aliaski do Ognennoi zemli [From Alaska to Tierra del
Fuego] (Moscow, 1967), pp. 136-141, for a description of
the entire work. Khlebnikov's "Statisticheskiia
svedeniia o koloniiakh Rossiisko-Amerikanskoi Kompanii"
[Statistical information on the colonies of the Russian-
American Company], Kommercheskaia gazeta, No. 80, 81, 87,
90, 93, 96, 98, 99, July-August, 1834, has been translated by James R. Gibson, as "Russian America in 1833:
An Official Profile," Pacific Northwest Quarterly,
January 1972, Vol. 63, No. 1, pp. 1-13.

Khlebnikov's Zhizneopisanie Aleksandra Andreevicha
Baranova, Glavnago Pravitelia Rossiiskikh Kolonii v
Amerike (Life of Aleksandr Andreevich Baranov, Chief
Manager of the Russian Colonies in America) is a record
of a man and a dream of empire. Baranov (1747-1818) is
one of the outstanding figures in the settlement of
North America by Europeans. John Smith, Peter Stuyve-
sant, Count Frontenac, Daniel Boone, Father Junipero
Serra and Baranov--all in their own way laid the found-
ations for civilized communities. Posterity may
criticize their methods, or question their right to the
lands they appropriated, but they and others set the
pattern of life for future generations.

Khlebnikov admits that he was not trained as a
writer. His simple, uncritical account omits many
details which we would like to have. Thus, he tells
nothing of Baranov's family, origins, youth and early
career, and barely mentions the wife and family Baranov
left in Russia, and his second wife, from a Kenai tribe,
and their two children. He purposely omits other
details which might have been unfavorable to his subject
or to the Company, giving a false picture of harmony be-

tween Baranov and the Orthodox missionaries who came
to Kad'iak in 1794, and providing no hint of the
quarrel between Baranov and Lieutenant M. D. Lazarev of
the Suvorov, whose report upon his return to St. Petersburg led to the Main Office to send out Captain Hagemeister to replace Baranov. Nevertheless, he provides
many details about Baranov which might otherwise have
been lost, and his account is of particular value because he knew his subject and served for years where he
could observe at first hand the effects of Baranov's
work. This work was an essential source for H. H.
Bancroft's classic History of Alaska (San Francisco,
1885), and Hector Chevigny's popular biographies Lost
Empire: The Life and Adventures of Nikolai Petrovich
Rezanov (New York, 1937) and Lord of Alaska: Baranov
and the Russian Venture (New York, 1942), and the survey Russian America, The Great Alaskan Venture, 1741-
1867 (New York, 1965).

For transliteration of Russian names and terms to
Latin script I have used a modified version of the
Library of Congress system. Hawaiian names have been
changed to fit modern usage. Thus, Kamehameha instead
of Tomea-mea, Kaumualii instead of Tomari. The forms
used by Khlebnikov are shown in brackets in the Index.
On the other hand designations "Americans" for both
North American natives and New England traders,
"Kolosh," for the Tlingit, "New Albion" for northern
California, and "Sandwich Islands" for the Hawaiian
Islands are retained. Western, rather than Russified
forms are used for Germanic names such as Krusenstern
and Hagemeister, instead of "Kruzenshtern" and
"Gagemeister." Most Russian ship names have been re-
tained, as Otkrytie (Discovery), but names similar to
European forms have been given as such, for example
Maria and Olga, instead of the more exact transliter-
ations Mariia and Ol'ga. Dates are as in the original
text. The Old Style (Julian) calendar then used in

Russia was twelve days behind the New Style (Gregorian) calendar, and in Russian America there was the added complication that as the International Date Line had not yet been conceived, eastbound ships failed to drop a day, and the Russian colonies remained only eleven days behind.

The Table of Contents is similar to the original, but with insertion of dates, and names of ships and masters. Editorial insertions have been made in brackets ([]). Several obvious printing errors have been corrected. Khlebnikov's notes have been placed at the end of the book, along with additional material.

For their help in various phases of this work I wish to thank Colin Bearne, of the University of Sussex, Denise Bearne, Joan Harcourt, Dalton Barber, and Laura Baldwin. Ross Hough of the Queen's University Cartographic Laboratory made the maps.

Richard A. Pierce

Queen's University
Kingston, Ontario
Canada

DEDICATION

To His Worship
the Admiral, Member of the State Council, and Chevalier
Of All Russian Orders,
COUNT NIKOLAI SEMENOVICH MORDVINOV

Most Excellent Count

Gracious Sire!

Being in the service of the Russian-American Company
from the beginning of the present century, I was sent in
1816 from St. Petersburg to the colonies as a commissioner aboard the ship Kutuzov. There I had the good
fortune to meet the honorable Aleksandr Andreevich
Baranov. I got to know him personally, and when I had
delivered our cargo and accepted from him the Company
funds, I met him every day.

After Aleksandr Andreevich was replaced I had the
honor to serve as manager of the Novo-Arkhangel'sk
office from the beginning of 1818 to the end of 1832,
and in dealings with the other offices and branches I
gradually learned of his many activities and plans. I
saw everywhere the results of his inexhaustible labors
and his efforts to bring profit and benefit to the
Company.

Baranov's worthy successors often wished to know
how things had been done in his time, and I had the
pleasure of providing them with such information. The
present Chief Manager, Baron Wrangel, has special respect for the memory of his works and expressed the wish
that a description of Baranov's deeds which were worthy

of attention and praise should be made for the general enlightenment of all. This was initially sufficient encouragement for me, and once I had collected some material, I set to work.

I was not trained as a writer and I am conscious of my own failings as a depicter of the deeds and exploits which the first Chief Manager of the colonies of the Russian-American Company achieved over the course of some 28 years; they deserve a better pen than mine, yet my heartfelt wish and obligation to express fully my gratitude to the worthy members of the Russian-American Company gave me strength and encouragement. The description of deeds performed in places where I had spent many years in Company service was a source of pleasant memories for me as I wrote them on the sea voyage home from the colonies.

Let us hope that this weak biography of the highly respected Baranov will be at least a temporary memorial to him, and a permanent sign of my recognition and gratitude to the staff of the Russian-American Company and of my deep respect and admiration for Your Honor's person as the foremost member of His Majesty's Council.

With these sentiments I have the honor to remain,

        Most Excellent Count and Gracious Sire,

        Your most humble servant

        Kiril Khlebnikov

St. Petersburg
April
1835

FOREWORD

There are in my possession letters written in Baranov's own hand to various people, his superiors in the Service. Using these and other materials I have described his business undertakings and administration. I am aware that my knowledge and capabilities are too limited and inadequate for this task, for to produce a full description I should have to write a history of the establishment and building up of the Company's colonies in America between 1790 and 1818. This is the period during which Baranov was acting solely on his own initiative, and generally alone. To write such a history one would need the abilities of an historian. I wish to preserve and leave some materials for future observers, and, in keeping them from being destroyed or forgotten, to present a record of actions and heroic achievements which, without any doubt, deserve the attention of the Fatherland and especially of the Russian-American Company.

I have based this biography on events, and often their description has been reinforced by eye-witness accounts from original letters and manuscripts. Rumors and the stories of associates have served only as confirmation.

It must be noted that Baranov was subject to the lot of any well known person; derogatory rumors and even envy marked his actions and deeds. But time and subsequent events have justified them and now it is already possible to talk boldly in a just and unprejudiced way about his rising posthumous reputation. The life of this citizen is not only memorable and interesting, but instructive for those who esteem people who are genuinely useful to their Fatherland irrespective of their origins.

A. A. Baranov

G. I. Shelikhov

N. P. Rezanov

I. A. Kuskov

Three Saints Bay, Kodiak Island, 1790

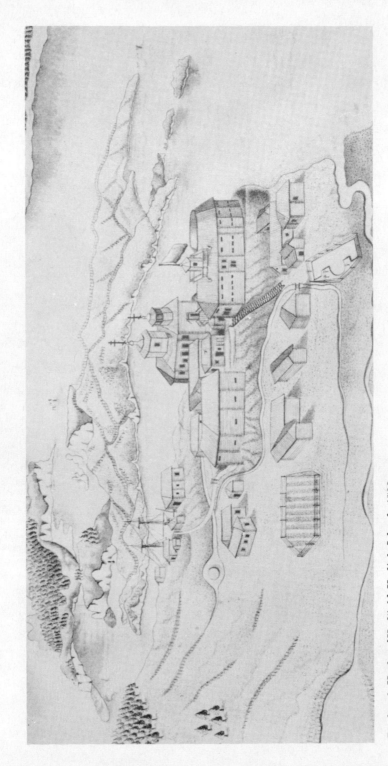

Pavlovsk Harbor [Kad'iak] Kodiak Island, 1798

Novo-Arkhangel'sk, 1805

Fort Ross in 1817

THE LIFE OF ALEKSANDR ANDREEVICH BARANOV

I would honor those
Who by their own effort
Have won titles
By praiseworthy deeds;
Who ungraced by family or fortune
Have by their valor earned
The esteem of the citizenry

Derzhavin

CHAPTER I

Aleksandr Andreevich Baranov, sometime merchant in
the town of Kargopol', engaged in trade in Moscow and
St. Petersburg until 1780, when he set out for Siberia.
Settling in Irkutsk, he managed glass factories and
vodka distilleries, and engaged in contracting and tax-
farming. In the course of his new activities he
acquired much valuable knowledge, and conveyed some of
his economic observations and experience to the Free
Economic Society, of which he was elected a member in
1787.

G. I. Shelikhov, who had just returned from a
journey to the coast of America, was looking for a
worthy and capable man to administer the colony which
he had established on Kad'iak. He offered the position
to Baranov, but because of his complex trade undertakings, the latter was compelled to refuse this offer.

In the following year Baranov's tax-farming and
contracting business in various places in Irkutsk
Gubernia took a turn for the worse and caused him heavy
losses. In the spring of 1790 he set out for Iakutsk,
and there found that his liquor tax-farming was likewise in disarray. In addition to his Siberian trade

he also participated in distant trading relations with
the Chukchi, who could obtain Russian goods by barter
at Izhiginsk. His agent on the Izhiga River came to
Okhotsk every year to go over the accounts and to
deliver furs. Baranov then went to Okhotsk intending
to set his affairs in order with the profits from his
Anadyrsk trade. But when he arrived he received sad
news. The settlement at Anadyrsk had been wiped out by
the Chukchi; the prikashchik and his employees were
dead and the stores had been plundered.

The disaster finally made Baranov receptive to
Shelikhov's repeated offers and he agreed to set out
for America. He left behind in Kargopol' his wife and
children and sent considerable sums of money yearly for
their upkeep.

Baranov and Shelikhov agreed that for administering
the colonies he would receive ten complete portions,
then called <u>sukhovye</u> shares, which in the division of
profits were paid in furs.[1]

On August 19, 1790 he put to sea in the galiot
<u>Three Saints</u>, [Tri Sviatitelia], under Navigator
Bocharov, the ablest seafarer in those parts.[2]

Shortly after they had left the port of Okhotsk it
was discovered that the fresh water barrels were leaking,
so each man's ration was reduced to four cups every 24
hours. On September 4 Baranov passed the first Kurile
strait and, although they should have sailed straight
on to Kad'iak, the lack of water began to cause sick-
ness among the 52-man crew. For this reason he decided
to put into Unalashka and on September 28 the ship
stood at anchor in Koshigin Bay.

After taking on fresh water they were ready to sail
on the 30th. But on the evening of that day a storm
blew up. The vessel dragged her anchor and ran aground;
the violent blows presaged all the horrors of shipwreck. All through a stormy and gloomy night, heavy
waves broke one after another on deck, the hatches were

ripped away, and the ship began to fill with water. In the face of such destruction the only course was to save the crew. At the morning low tide they hurriedly unloaded what cargo they could onto the shore before the tide came in. The storm did not die down and on the night of October 6 the ship capsized completely. A little of the Company cargo was salvaged but Baranov, the crew and the passengers were left destitute.

Aleksandr Molev was sent to Kad'iak to convey the news of their misfortunes and to seek help. On the Alaska Peninsula, about 100 versts short of Kad'iak, he was attacked by the Alaskans. Five of the Fox Island Aleuts accompanying him were killed, and he [and the others] after a lengthy exchange of fire, escaped by sea in baidarkas, reached the island of Unga and remained there until Baranov arrived.

Thus the hopes of help from Kad'iak were in vain. Baranov sent people to various parts of the island to shoot seals and sea lions and to gather roots for sustenance during the coming winter. Misfortune is a great leveller of men. Like his fellow voyagers he lived in a hastily constructed yurt dug out of the earth, and kept alive by eating various grasses, roots, whale meat and crabs. Iukola (dried fish) which they received from the Aleuts was a delicacy for them. They had luxuries only on holidays; then they would make a thin broth out of rye flour; this the workers called zaturan and shared it out in equal portions.

Baranov, describing his condition says:

> I passed the winter in a state of great boredom, especially when the weather was bad. Sometimes storms would set in for two whole months and it would be impossible to go out anywhere. But on the other hand we did not let a single fine day go by without going out with our guns, which provided us with a plentiful supply of food. On one of these walks I fell into some snares set for foxes and injured myself, but not seriously.

In another letter to his friends he wrote:

I boiled salt myself, as white as snow,
and sometimes we would salt fish or seal
or sea lion flesh with it. At Lent we all
fasted a proper fast and on Whit Monday
part of a whale was washed up and we broke
our fast with that. During the first week
we killed three sea lions and after that
wanted for nothing. I no longer think
about either bread or sugar.

Acquainting himself with the country and its
population, Baranov worked out plans for administering
the colonies and presented them to Shelikhov, seeking
his opinions and advice. Like a true son of the Church
and the Fatherland, he proposed first of all to
enlighten the savages with the Light of the Gospel,
since he was convinced that a good pastor, having
studied the native tongue, could, by the teaching of
the Everlasting Word and the example of a righteous
Christian life, more successfully inculcate in them a
sense of work and community. He therefore requested
"Send a wise priest, a humble man and not superstitious
or hypocritical." He wanted to influence the natives
not by fear and threats but with gentle consideration
for their obdurate ignorance, and fully understanding
the childish wishes of the savages, who were intrigued
by glittering baubles, he intended to gain their
loyalty with gifts. Since many articles would be
needed to pursue this end, he wrote to Shelikhov;

All else may seem superfluous and unnecessary to you, but under the circumstances I should like to take the risk on
my own account. If such a plan is
rewarded then I can turn it to the good of
the Company, claiming back only the cost
of the articles involved; if the plan fails
then the loss will be mine. I want to gain
the goodwill of these wild Americans by
making them gifts, even in the most
dangerous undertakings. Near Chugatsk Bay
I propose to construct a vessel, in order
thus to set up friendly relations with the
local people which may be profitable to
the Company. We shall not interfere with
them nor give them the slightest reason

for bitterness, and after a while I hope
simply to gain their support. Once the ship
has been built I want to follow the Northwest Coast [southward] until I reach a
European settlement and only then to turn
north. Such is my plan at the moment, but
its execution is dependent upon Providence.
My first steps here were visited with misfortune by a cruel fate, but perhaps the
end of my endeavours will be crowned with
generous good fortune, or I shall fall under
the burden of Fate's blows. Privation and
boredom I can bear with patience and I shall
not rant at Providence, especially when I
sacrifice to friendship.

With the coming of spring, measures were taken for
the crossing to Kad'iak; three large leather baidaras
were built and it was decided that Navigator Bocharov
should take two with 26 men and set off to chart the
north coast of the Alaska Peninsula. Baranov was to
take 16 men with him, and five men were chosen to guard
the cargo and tackle left on Unalashka.

On April 25, 1791, all the baidaras set out and on
May 10 they parted in Isannakh Strait according to the
prearranged plan. On this journey Baranov was ill with
a fever for two months, but the expedition continued
nevertheless. They did not want to lose the calm
weather which was so suitable for crossing from island
to island or going between the capes along the coast of
Alaska. They reached Kad'iak on June 27.

Bocharov, on his journey along the north side of
the peninsula, described what he saw, and made plans
and maps. He intended to sail further along the
Aglegmiut coast, but it transpired that the baidaras
had rotted[3] and could hardly be used: for this reason
on August 11 they began to carry the baidaras to the
other side of the peninsula through the mountains.
This was accomplished in three days, and, when the
baidaras had been repaired, they crossed to the island
of Kad'iak on the 27th and on September 12 reached the
harbor there.[4]

At this time Shelikhov's company occupied Kad'iak

Island and the adjoining islands, whose inhabitants had
been made Russian subjects. The main settlement was on
Kad'iak at Three Saints Bay. After Shelikhov's
departure the inhabitants of this island were no longer
rebellious and having given hostages, they lived peace-
fully. Yet, they remained in the same savage state in
which Shelikhov had found them and could only be kept
subservient by force and fear. Given the least slip by
the Russians, they would not have missed an opportunity
to kill them all to a man. The manager Delarov had
sent a detachment from Kad'iak to the American mainland
near the entrance to Kenai Bay where the Aleksandrovsk
fort had been founded. The inhabitants of the Alaska
Peninsula were hostile and would not allow settlement.
Among the islands of the Aleutian chain there were in
various places groups from private companies, of the
merchants Orekhov from Tula, Panov from Vologda, and
Kiselev from Irkutsk. Agents of the Iakutsk merchant
Lebedev-Lastochkin had occupied Kenai Bay, and the
mariner Pribylov on one of Lebedev's ships had discovered the uninhabited seal islands Paul and George.
With the exception of Lebedev, none of the private
companies had permanently settled bases, and since they
came only temporarily for furs they were not concerned
about educating the inhabitants or about their own
personal safety. By using all possible means to increase trade they often abused the natives. This is
described by Admiral I. F. Krusenstern in the introduction to his voyage,

> The extraordinary increase in traders
> brought with it evil consequences which,
> without the intervention of the merchant
> Shelikhov, who laid the foundations of the
> present American Company, would soon have
> destroyed any profitable trading altogether.
> Each vessel setting off to trap animals
> belonged to a specific master, who thought
> neither of sparing the Aleut nor the
> animals which would bring him wealth; in a
> word, they did not think about the future,
> but only of how to fill up their boats as

soon as possible, by whatever means, and of
the return journey to Okhotsk. Such a
wholesale devastation threatened to make
sea otters and other animals extinct within
a very short time; the trade would have
come to an end, or at least would have
ceased for a long time. Shelikhov, who saw
the need to limit this destructive kind of
trading, tried to get the participants to
form into a society, so that their
activities might be planned.[5]

Shelikhov's idea was well-founded. He planned to
make the savage inhabitants Russian subjects, and to
teach them a settled life not by force of arms, but by
awakening their enthusiasm for fur hunting by the
conditions and pay. The Greek E. I. Delarov was then
manager of the colony on Kad'iak; from him Baranov took
over all the estates and capital.[6]

In the following year, 1792, Delarov returned to
the port of Okhotsk on the ship Sv. Mikhail under the
command of Bocharov and brought with him some selected
fur goods. Baranov, when he had examined various
localities on Kad'iak Island, recognised the necessity
of moving the settlement to the port of Pavlovsk
[Paul's Harbor] (latitude 57°36' and longitude 152°8'
according to Captain Lisianskii's observations). Since
the place was surrounded by forests, he was able to
build comfortable homes and service buildings; then he
busied himself with extending the settlement and
developing the sea otter trade, for which purpose he
dispatched large parties of Aleuts to Kenai Bay and
along the Alaska [Peninsula] coast. There were
altogether about 150 Russian promyshlenniks in America,
mainly peasants and townsmen from various gubernias.
Most were free men, not used to obedience and order,
and rather coarse and ignorant; but amongst them there
were some with good natural capabilities, who only had
to be prodded, trained and used to advantage. The seafarer Izmailov of the Okhotsk command, who was in the
colony, was sent to discover islands of whose existence

there was only untrustworthy evidence. Passing several
times in various directions those points where the
islands were presumed to be, he was able to demonstrate
that reports of their existence were false.

Baranov himself set out in two baidaras for Chugatsk
Bay, to meet the inhabitants and build a settlement
there. The Chugach are a warlike people, and savage,
but taking fright at the appearance of the Russians and
their companions, they hid from Baranov everywhere. He
did manage to meet some tribes, however, and took from
them seven hostages (amanats). Baranov found here the
East-Indiaman Phoenix whose captain, one Moore, met
Baranov and made him a present of a Bengal Indian.

One day they stopped opposite Sukli [Montague]
Island. Baranov sent off a baidara to look it over and
while he awaited the return of the party he and his men
pitched tents at the water's edge and prepared for
sleep. In the middle of the night, in the pitch dark
when all were asleep, the desperate shout of the guard
caused sudden alarm as the savages attacked. The
Russians grabbed their rifles in the darkness and drove
off the attackers. They met with stiff resistance yet
did not know with whom they were fighting. Their
daring enemies were Yakutat Kolosh who had come ashore
under cover of darkness looking for the Chugach when
they suddenly came upon the Russians. The Kolosh were
wearing war dress consisting of wooden armor tightly
wound about with whale-gut. Their faces were covered
with masks made to resemble the faces of bears, seals,
and other animals striking for their fearsome appearance. On their heads they had tall, thick wooden hats
joined to their other clothing with straps. Their
weapons consisted of spears, arrows, and two-ended
daggers. The Russians aimed mostly for their heads, but
the bullets passed harmlessly through the tall hats.
The more they fired their guns, the more wildly ever new
waves of attackers would rush forward. The Russians·

were few in number and their strength weakened considerably until only half remained alive. On the other hand the desperate desire grew either to avenge their dead comrades or to fall on the bodies of their host of enemies. Once the Kolosh had met such a strong answering fire from the rifles, they eventually began to fall back. Although they had superior numbers (not less than five to one) and the advantage of a sudden attack on sleeping men, they could not hold the upper hand and gave way to flight.

Subsequently Baranov, when reporting the incident to Shelikhov, wrote:

> Two of my Russians were killed and ten Aleuts, but though I only had 15 men left, with God's help I broke up and drove off the attackers, protected with wood, and defended by much armor; there were six baidaras full of warriors, and they attacked in the middle of the night but they were spotted by the guard. We kept firing at them for three hours, until we had driven them away. Twelve of the Kolosh died on the spot, but the bloodstains stretching away for a verst showed that they had lost more men. Although they had arrived in six baidaras, they left in only five.

Of the seven Chugach hostages mentioned above, four escaped when the alarm was first sounded. They thought it was their fellow-tribesmen attacking, but because of their mistake, they were captured and taken off by the Kolosh. Several wounded Kolosh remained as prisoners of Baranov. It was from them that he learned that the Kolosh had arrived in six baidaras intending to kill all the Chugach and then turn their attention to the Russian settlements. At this news he hurriedly set off for the Kenai settlement and there took the necessary measures for strengthening the defences. From there he returned to Kad'iak where meantime the packet-boat _Orel_ had arrived from Okhotsk. On it was the Englishman Shields, who had previously served as a lieutenant in

the Ekaterinburg regiment, but since he was a shipwright and a seafarer Shelikhov had made an agreement
with him and accepted him for service in the new
colonies. The first proof of Shields' abilities was
the Orel, which he had built in Okhotsk.

During that year Baranov travelled by baidara all
around Kad'iak Island, inspecting all the Russian
settlements and arranging to assign men for hunting sea
otters.

In the following year, 1793, Baranov travelled by
baidara around Kenai Bay, chose a harbor in Chugatsk
Bay which had a plentiful supply of wood for shipbuilding, and ordered that a ship be built there. This
port was named Voskresensk. Shields came from Kad'iak
by boat, with craftsmen and materials. A serious
difficulty was a lack of tar and pitch; instead pine
and fir sap were collected which, when boiled together,
produced a gum fit for use in shipbuilding. On the
return journey from Voskresensk Bay, Baranov was long
delayed by storms and it was November before he reached
Kad'iak. Travelling at this late season, around
latitude 60° North, on the open sea, in wind, rain,
hail and snow, with short daylight, and in weak boats
like leather baidaras is in itself dangerous, and can
often be fatal. It could have been considered quite
ordinary and normal if on the journey there had been
peaceful shelter and warm food, but in practice the
winds would often hold boats on barren, treeless and
rocky shores, where the travellers sheltered themselves
from the damp, storm and cold in nothing but upturned
baidaras. Often they were hungry and cold, and had to
consume shellfish they gathered from the beach at low
tide. Among these there would often be poisonous ones,
and instead of the joys of slaking one's hunger there
would be cramps and convulsions and the death which
usually followed would itself be accounted a joyous
release. Once on the American mainland it was always

necessary to be wary of attacks from the hostile
inhabitants. This depiction is a true one, yet it is
still not harsh enough to convey all the difficulties
and obstacles which had to be contended with at that
time.

In the first two years of Baranov's administration
the trade volume was 2,150 sea otter skins which were
divided up into 210 equal parts or shares.

It must be noted here that in this description the
inhabitants of Kad'iak, the Kenais, the Chugach, and
others sent off in groups for hunting sea otters are
referred to under the general title of Aleuts, although
in a geographic sense this is inappropriate. In fact
'Aleuts' can only be applied to inhabitants of the
Aleutian islands--that is the nearer groups, the
Andreianov and Fox Islands. The Kad'iaks call themselves Koniagas, whilst the inhabitants of Alaska,
Kenai Bay and so forth should be distinguished by the
name of their habitation. Yet in the trading business
this difference is irrelevant and a general name has
been adopted.

CHAPTER II

When the colony on Kad'iak was founded, Shelikhov's
goals were the broadening of the frontiers of Russia,
the subjugation of hitherto unknown savage peoples and
the development of the trade in sea otter pelts. This
latter goal was a method of achieving the first two,
for without a considerable trade there would be no way
for the authorities to act successfully, or those be-
neath them, willingly. Each of the latter, considering
himself a participant, would boldly take part in the
most daring enterprises; it is easy to lead such
people and achieve the aim set out.

In the first years of Baranov's term in office
sea otter hunting went on in Kenai and Chugatsk Bays,
but then they found the number of sea otter there
sharply decreasing. Early in 1794 Baranov therefore
equipped an expedition to explore Yakutat Bay under
the leadership of his deputies Purtov and Kulikalov.
He himself set off in baidaras to Chugatsk Bay to
attend to duties amongst the local population and to
strengthen his expedition with Chugach. Five hundred
baidarkas joined it and reached Yakutat safely. There
he found the famous English Captain Vancouver, who saw
the expedition and received its leaders hospitably.
When he had gleaned from them information which he
needed[8] he met Baranov alone and later filled several
sheets of his journal with his name and deeds.[9]

While Baranov was at Voskresensk Harbor, a three-
masted ship was built, launched, and christened the
Phoenix. This was the first ship built by the
Russians in America. It gave Baranov real pleasure to
see timber from this far-off American wilderness being
used for the good of the fatherland, and lack of

12

materials and other handicaps overcome. Such a feeling
is a pleasure so great that it is difficult to convey
to others who have never dealt with such matters. But
those who have will appreciate his satisfaction.

The _Phoenix_, under command of Shields, arrived in
Kad'iak on September 4, while Baranov returned thence in
a baidarka.

In autumn two transports arrived from Okhotsk, the
first being the _Three Saints_ under command of
Navigator Izmailov. This ship brought the Archimandrite
Ioasaf with a retinue of ten clerics, sent on Imperial
orders to spread the Word of God to the people who had
come under the rule of the Russian State.[10] The other
transport was the _Ekaterina_ under command of Navigator
Pribylov. These two vessels brought with them 130
promyshlenniks, amongst whom were 30 settler families.
These were craftsmen and farmers, given at the wish of
the Monarch to Shelikhov, so that the colonies might
benefit from their trades. The Governor-General of
Irkutsk, Pil', directed Shelikhov to settle them near
Cape St. Elias, or wherever was most suitable for their
establishment. It is impossible to approve of
Shelikhov's proposal to settle America with criminals,
for these people, having lost their good name in Russia
and having sunk into depravity during exile, could be
and were in fact most harmful to the colony due to
their base morals.

The brig _Ekaterina_ sailed into Unalashka to dis-
charge some of her cargo there and on the return
journey, in Akutan Strait, she met a fierce storm with
a strong _suloi_ or tide rip.[11] Part of the cargo was
lost and several head of horned cattle, but some were
brought to Kad'iak and since then have been shared out
throughout the colonies.

In the stormy autumn of that year a baidara with 14
Russians aboard, returning from Kenai Bay with a cargo
of pelts, went down in a gale. At that time it was not

possible to avoid this danger because of the lack of
sailing vessels. Everyone could see the hazards, but in
more than one journey between the islands others
suffered the same fate.

Not far from Kad'iak is the small wooded island of
Elovoi [Spruce], where, for convenience, Baranov proposed to build two small sailing vessels: this work
was allocated to Shields. During 1795 both vessels, 35
to 40 feet in keel length, were completed and named the
Del'fin [Dolphin] and the Olga. That summer the ship
Phoenix set out for Okhotsk under the command of
Izmailov. On this ship Baranov, reporting on his
administration, wrote to Shelikhov:

> My affairs will reveal to you that even if
> my administration of the office is not of the
> best, then at least it is not the worst: I
> myself don't touch a thread nor a hair. I
> don't hesitate to give of my own to good and
> trusted and energetic employees, be they
> Russians, foreigners or hostages. Thus it
> would seem that you have absolutely no reason
> to complain of unnecessary expenses.

Yet from their correspondence at that time it is
even more noticeable that when Baranov received critical
inquiry from Shelikhov he would try to smooth it over
and in order to refute the slander he would say, with
great sincerity:

> About the rumors which have come to your
> ears from promyshlenniks leaving these parts
> I do not much care. Let me point to my
> actual achievements. Has all my time here
> been exercised in idleness and depravity?
> If you ask idlers and good-for-nothings they
> will tell you nothing good about me because
> I have been hard on them. But if you ask
> the industrious and those who really perform
> worthwhile services for the company then you
> will hear a different story.[12]

Reporting further on his explorations and projects
he writes:

> Iron ores have been discovered in quite
> large quantities and as an experiment iron

has been melted and thus the prospect is open for us to open iron works for the benefit of the Fatherland.

The expedition sent to Yakutat in 1794 found many sea otters. There and on the journey almost 2,000 were processed. Yakutat Bay, which Cook called Bering Bay, was surveyed and described in 1788 by the seafarers Izmailov and Bocharov, sent from Kad'iak by the manager Delarov.[13] Purtov, a deputy attached to the expedition, had amassed much information about the bay and Baranov decided to build a settlement there. It was a more suitable place in many ways than Cape St. Elias which Shelikhov had suggested, and whence as an experiment a small artel had been sent. Because of the convenient harbor, a settlement at Yakutat would be a stores depot for expeditions sent on sea otter hunts, even along the mainland coast of America to the southeast. Shields was sent on one of the newly built vessels to survey the shore from the Queen Charlotte Islands as far as Edgecumbe, and from there to proceed to Yakutat to join forces with the manager.

A hunting expedition of baidarkas under the command of Purtov and Kondakov was to go on the usual route to Yakutat, and even farther if possible. The vessel Three Saints under Pribylov was sent straight to Yakutat; on board were 20 settler families and 30 promyshlenniks who were to form a settlement under the direction of Polomoshnoi, who had been sent by Shelikhov specially to do this. From the spiritual mission Hieromonk Juvenal was sent along to convert the savages.

After sending off this expedition Baranov sailed in June on the galley Olga straight to Yakutat. Since he had some knowledge of seamanship, he was himself commander and navigator of the little vessel. On the third day out they arrived at their destination where they were greeted by the Kolosh in a very hostile fashion. The hunting expedition which had been there before him had also been threatened by the Kolosh, so

had not stopped there, but continued along the coast.
Baranov, recording this incident, writes:

> Our party in Yakutat were afraid of the
> Kolosh, thus giving them reason to think us
> cowards. However, we showed them that even
> with our small numbers they were deceived if
> they placed their hope in rifles bartered from
> foreigners. We challenged them to test their
> strength and luck against us, and I showed
> them by the swiftness and accuracy of our
> weapons how few people were needed. After
> that we began to live with them on friendly
> terms.

Expecting the vessel <u>Three Saints</u>, Baranov remained
in Yakutat until August 15. Finally, feeling he had
waited too long, he resolved to go, leaving behind a few
Russians and Kad'iaks to reinforce the expedition. For
their protection he persuaded the Kolosh toens to give
some of their relatives as hostages. Taking these on
board he set out to sea and, navigating by the shoreline, approached the ice floe and the Chastye Islands.
Autumn was near, strong east winds were starting to
blow, and so they returned on September 8. Since they
were unable to reach Yakutat they stopped at the Kenai
settlement.

At the same time Hieromonk Juvenal arrived in the
settlement from Nuchek. He brought with him the news
that the <u>Three Saints</u> had put in to Nuchek for fresh
water and after taking barrels on board she had returned
to Kad'iak. Baranov well knew the supply of water, the
number of people, and the length of time the crossing
should take, and therefore he had no doubt that
Polomoshnoi's intrigues were the cause of it all. The
latter had earlier disagreed with Baranov during the
building of the settlement in Yakutat. It should be
noted here that Juvenal, fervent in spreading God's
Word, turned north from there to the savage Aglegmiuts,
with nothing but his faith, and we do not know for
certain where he died at their hands.

On October 1 Baranov reached Kad'iak where he found

Shields, who reported that from Port Bucarelli he had
inspected various places along the coast and throughout
the voyage had seen many sea otters. He had made lists
and charts of all the coastlines he had explored.

Baranov, who had travelled all over the Northwest
Coast of America, had got to know several tribes of
Kolosh. He learnt that these peoples had many children,
were strong, savage, and because they were attracted to
barter and trade they soon became hard-working traders.
They were able to adopt European customs and with their
innate intelligence and ability they soon learnt how to
fire guns. He foresaw that it would not be easy to
occupy their territories and it would need a great
effort to subdue them. But the more obstacles and
difficulties there arose, the stronger burned his desire
to overcome them and to achieve the proposed goal. For
people who are firm in their decisions, there is a
general axion: the worse the better! and for a quick
and active mind to be without work is to be without
pleasure.

As evidence of Baranov's farsighted designs, I
introduce a very striking exposition of his ideas from
one of his addresses to the Company:

> There are many places in America beyond
> Yakutat which, for the good of the Fatherland,
> ought to have been occupied by Russians long
> ago, instead of Europeans, amongst whom the
> English have set up a very profitable trade on
> those shores as far as Nootka itself. Several
> of their ships arrive each year--they pay the
> Americans very generously for their products.
> They exchange a great many rifles and cart-
> ridges, which the natives are very proud of.
> But good spirits and fearlessness are needed
> to overcome the initial difficulties,
> qualities which one hopes it will always be
> possible to find in the Russian people. To
> settle America as far as Nootka and thereby
> bring honor to the Fatherland is a deed worthy
> of praise. To the Fatherland we are duty
> bound to sacrifice our peace and life both by
> our oath of allegiance and our conscience.

From these brief and lucid thoughts is revealed

a spirit both decisive and bold, thirsting to bring profit and fame to the Fatherland, and to share the honor of participating in acquiring a significant stretch of territory and subduing savage yet bold and well-armed peoples.

Had he been given the material means to accompany this enthusiasm, then he would have been able to act with appropriate speed. But left to himself with insufficient reserves of men, ships, guns and cartridges, he was forced to delay his schemes and to settle places on the American coast gradually and with a small force. In this situation it seemed as though he were feeling his way forward, looking round cautiously.

Meanwhile, a church had been built on Kad'iak. Baranov was well pleased to have the Archimandrite Ioasaf as a companion, and contented with his instruction. He paid just compliment to his enlightened mind, his quiet manner, and his kind heart. Wishing to help with the business of conversion, he himself made contributions, or, as he explains, "Overjoyed in spirit at the good news of the Holy Gospel brought here, I, in my zeal offered for the use of the Church and clergy one thousand five hundred rubles from myself, and five hundred rubles from various employees."[14]

Baranov had as yet no accurate information about the total population of Kad'iak, and so in December he set off in a baidara to go right around the island. On this journey he took an accurate census. He also made arrangements for the sea otter hunting expeditions, and gave fresh instructions to the heads of artels living in various places. He returned to Pavlovsk Harbor on March 9, 1796. The following figures emerged from the Kad'iak census: 3,221 males, 2,985 females, making a total population of 6,206. There were as many as seven hundred baidarkas engaged in sea otter hunting.

At the request of Koch, the Commandant of Okhotsk, Baranov gave him detailed lists of the populations on Unalashka and the other islands. Observing the morals,

customs and ways of the Aleuts, he thoroughly and
lucidly described them. Amongst the items of information conveyed to Koch was the fact that in 1788 an
English ship arrived at Atkha Island. The Captain, Cox,
was said to have parted from the Russians on very bad
terms.

Soon after this the seafarer Pribylov died, but
Baranov did not postpone his expedition to Yakutat. The
baidarshchik Medvednikov volunteered to command the ship,
taking as assistant his apprentice Kashevarov, who had
sailed several times with Shields. The same people were
sent to build a settlement under the command of manager
Polomoshnoi, with Stepan Larionov as assistant.

The packet-boat Orel, with Shields in command, was
also sent to Yakutat as a reinforcement, and a party of
450 baidarkas was instructed to proceed as far as L'tua
Bay. In addition, in 1796, 112 baidarkas were
requisitioned from the islands for sea otter hunting
and 145 from Alaska. Men setting out in baidarkas
stocked up with iukola in the Karluk settlement, placing
from 100 to 125 fish in each. The Aleuts only used this
stock in emergency. On the journey itself, at every
possible stop they would catch fish, and shoot birds,
hair seals or sea lions. Roots, shellfish and the meat
of sea-otters also went to make up the normal diet of
the Aleuts. They were born to it, but the Russians, for
lack of bread, had to eat the same.

Leaving the administration of Kad'iak, as he had
done before, in the hands of his assistant Kuskov,[15]
Baranov set off for Yakutat in the galley Olga. On the
way he called in at the settlement of Cape St. Elias
and on July 15 reached his destination. The ship Three
Saints had already been there since June 25. Baranov
found the people who had been left there the previous
year alive and well, but complaining that they had
several times gone short of food in the winter.

When they had chosen a suitable site for a settlement they set to building houses; Baranov stayed two

months until the building was completed. He accepted
11 new hostages from the Kolosh, left a garrison of 50
men and set sail again for Kad'iak.

The vessel Three Saints, dispatched from Yakutat on
September 2, was held up by storms in Kamyshatsk Bay
and there suffered serious damage. The party of Aleuts
had reached the shore of L'tua Bay under escort by the
Orel onto which all the sea otter pelts were taken—up
to 1800 skins—and the vessel proceeded to Sitka Bay to
reconnoiter. During that winter Ensign Rodionov
returned to Kad'iak by baidara from the new settlement
at Cape St. Elias with word that the lack of fish made
it impossible for the settlement to exist there.

After making the usual arrangements for the sea
otter hunts, Baranov, in June 1797 sent men to
Kamyshatsk Bay to repair the Three Saints, which had
been damaged there. But finding her already destroyed
they burned the remains for her iron. A section of this
party returned to Kad'iak and the others set off for
Lake Iliamna to build a settlement. Once there they
subdued the natives, who had been hostile until then,
and took hostages from them. Baranov himself went on
the galley Olga to Kenai Bay and then to Voskresensk
Harbor. There he learnt from people specially sent
from Yakutat in baidarkas that during the winter 20
workers and several women had died from scurvy. In
Chugatsk Bay he visited Konstantinovsk fort on Nuchek
Island where until then a party of Lebedev-Lastochkin's
company had been holding out. Because they had been
several years without replacement or reinforcements,
they had not only been useless to their company but
through the arrogance of their leader Konovalov,
quarrels and dissatisfaction arose amongst the hunters,
precipitating many crises. Because of this most of the
hunters entered Baranov's service there and then, while
the remainder were sent back to Okhotsk. The Chugach
dwelling on this bay also put themselves under Baranov's
command; he took their census and a hundred of their

baidarkas joined the hunting expedition.

Baranov was very happy to gain influence over this area. The Chugach are of the same origins as the people of Kad'iak, but because they are surrounded by peoples who are their historical enemies, they were subject to attack by the Kolosh from the sea and by the inhabitants of the Copper [Mednaia] River from land. They were therefore warlike, extremely wary, and energetic. When the first Russian ships visited their shores they were completely unapproachable; in 1783 they fell upon one of the Panov Company's ships and drove it off; they also resisted landing parties from Captain Billings' expedition in 1791. Admiral G. A. Sarychev relates in his journal how

> ...the savages, finding they had no opportunity to steal our beads, decided to kill us all at the first opportunity. They wanted to cut all our throats, as they had once done to some in-cautious Spaniards, who, as they themselves pointed out, were fishing unarmed and trusting them completely. On another occasion these savages (the Chugach) intended to attack us when we were dining with them in the strait.[16]

When Lebedev-Lastochkin's party ventured there, since they were quite strong and armed the Chugach offered resistance for some time, and it was only after more than one pitched battle that they were subdued.

While Baranov was staying here a fierce storm began on September 11 which raged for four days without a break and with violent thunder and lightning. As a result, in the countryside around the settlement, more than two hundred mature spruce trees were torn up by the roots and smashed to bits. Leaving the Konstant-inovsk redoubt on September 27 Baranov returned to Kad'iak on October 1, while the party of Aleuts escorted by the packet-boat Orel, under Shields' command, got as far as Sitka Bay. Their catch included 2,000 sea otter pelts.

During October the Phoenix arrived from Okhotsk. It was under command of Navigator 12th class Talin, who

was assigned from the fleet to the Company's service
on Imperial orders, together with Navigators Kolbin and
Pyshenkov, as was also Potash (Potach), a seafarer
summoned from Arkhangel'sk.

Baranov now received the sad news that G. I.
Shelikhov had died in Irkutsk on July 20, 1795.
Shelikhov's wife and his partner Golikov, who had begun
administering his affairs, joined with the Company of
Irkutsk merchants and with them sent a special letter
to Baranov. They informed him of events and asked him
to stay in America at least until the stockholder
Larionov, who had been sent from Unalashka as manager,
got to grips with affairs. Until then they promised to
follow his instructions.

The Irkutsk Company had existed even during
Shelikhov's lifetime, its aim being to foster trade in
the Aleutian chain from Kamchatka to Alaska. Its vessel,
the Zosima and Savatiia, which was under the command of
the old seafarer, Boatswain Sapozhnikov, was blown so
far south that the pitch between the planking started to
melt. The startled mariners, who had lost all idea of
their course, went with the wind and fortunately sailed
north. On October 6, 1797, they arrived at Afognak
Island without anchors or boats and only small reserves
of water and provisions.[17] Baranov gave them all the
help he could and provided an officer who guided them
into Unalashka, where meanwhile the stockholder Emel'ian
Larionov had arrived to take charge of the United
Company's affairs.

When sailing resumed in 1798 the ship Phoenix was
sent to Okhotsk under Shields. On board was Archimandrite Ioasaf who had been ordered to Irkutsk at the
Imperial behest, in order to be made a bishop. The
naval officers Pyshenkov and Kolbin also travelled with
Shields. The Company had instructed Baranov to send a
party of hunters and Aleuts to settle Urup, the
eighteenth island of the Kurile chain, but aiming at
more important and more useful ventures on the American

coast, he replied that it was not possible to carry
out these instructions. He suggested instead that the
Company headquarters in Okhotsk should be responsible,
since it was nearer.

On the vessel _Ekaterina_ under the command of Potash,
some horned cattle were sent to Yakutat for breeding.
Navigator Talin, on the _Orel_, was sent out to chart the
shoreline near Sitka. Baranov himself, on the galley
Olga, was travelling round all the settlements: first
he went to Kenai Bay, as he writes, "In order to pacify
the rebellious and mutinous people (the natives) who
had between them destroyed more than 100 lives and as
they grew in number began to threaten our settlement on
the river Ikatna." But even before he arrived there,
some of the Kenai people loyal to the Russians had
captured the rebels and handed some over as hostages
to the head of the Kenai settlement. "I stayed,"
continues Baranov, "until August 15, and arranging to
establish a serf settlement in another suitable and safe
place, I went through the various spots I knew and made
my plans according to the lay of the land. Then I
handed matters over to Malakhov, the man in charge."

Thence he travelled to Nuchek in Chugatsk Bay where
he examined the affairs of the Konstantinovsk fort, and
assessing their needs, suggested that the fort be re-
constructed on another site. Leaving his deputy Kuskov
in charge of this, he set off on the return journey on
September 25 and arrived back in Kad'iak on October 5.
The party of Aleuts under the guidance of Kandakov and
Dem'ianenkov went as far as Sitka Island; they had a
catch of more than a thousand sea otters, and returned
to Kad'iak with the loss of ten Aleuts who were drowned
off the Agalakhmiut coast.

From Nuchek, Baranov sent a Russian to the Copper
River to investigate that region and its products.

CHAPTER III

The fort established at Yakutat at Baranov's
direction was merely a gateway to the Northwest Coast of
America with its wealth in sea otters. From the rare
newspapers that he received he learnt that the Spanish
Court had ceded Nootka Sound (his goal) to the English.
When he received further information about this from
foreigners, he expressed his ideas on the subject to
the Company thus:

> At the moment there is no one at Nootka,
> neither English nor Spaniards; it has been left
> empty. When they arrive, however, they will of
> course attempt to spread their trading area and
> to stake a claim in our area. I have heard from
> the Americans that they intend to form a special
> company, to settle permanently near the Queen
> Charlotte Islands, in the direction of Sitka.
> Maybe the Imperial Court can grant us protection
> from interference with our trading and hunting
> by foreigners, if, that is, the Company's case
> can be well presented to the Throne. This could
> be very important at present, while Nootka is
> unoccupied by the English and while the [Spanish
> and English courts and the American republic]
> are at war with France. The benefits from those
> areas would be so important that I would hope
> the State would gain by millions in the future.
> One need only consider the fact that more than
> ten years have passed with six to ten English
> or American vessels visiting the place every
> year. Now if each vessel loads less than 1,500
> sea otter pelts they run at a loss, but at
> various places on that shoreline it is not un-
> usual to barter from two to three thousand.
> Say we take the middle figure of 2,000 for six
> ships per annum, then that gives us 12,000
> pelts, and again, even if we take the lower
> figure of 10,000, it follows that over ten
> years this becomes 100,000. If we then say that
> a sea otter changes hands in Canton for 45 rubles,
> that would be 4,500,000 rubles. Then take off
> 1,500,000 for expenses and stores, that leaves
> 3,000,000 rubles clear profit over ten years.
> These profits, in all justice and natural law,

should belong to Russian subjects alone. But
if we also add the fact that in Canton there
is a great deal of cheap "software" brought
in through various channels and that this
cheap jumble spreads all over China, then this
will make a great hole in our Kiakhta trade,
and in the end may be able to stop commerce
there altogether. The Americans tell me that
when our Kiakhta trade was closed they made
terrific profits and sold their imported
software for 20% more. From which it
follows that the produce of the Canton trade
influences the Kiakhta trade.[18] These same
compelling reasons, obliging me to serve the
Fatherland, stimulated me to set up the
settlement in Sitka in good time and to find
out how things stood locally, in Canton, and
with the visiting traders. I decided, whatever our weakness in numbers and conditions,
to set up at least some basic institutions
and acquaintances, and to wait for time to
bring fuller fruits. It would indeed be a
great shame, if Europeans or another company
should cut these places off from us. If that
were the case then all our successes hitherto
would be wiped out.

He drew attention mainly to Sitka Bay which he had
visited several times and found most suitable for
permanent settlement. The shoreline was more densely
populated than that of Yakutat and the people there had
long since been visited by Europeans and Americans.
They had thereby accumulated many rifles and from their
frequent intercourse with visitors they understood the
strength and weaknesses of peoples hitherto unknown to
them. Therefore more thoroughgoing measures had to be
adopted. To this end a party of 550 Aleut baidarkas
was fitted out. These, apart from their duties in sea
otter hunting, could, if need arose, help in occupying
the desired site. The vessel Ekaterina under command of
Potash was despatched thence with the materials needed
for building the new fort. He had been instructed to
call in at Yakutat on the way and then at the port of
Bucarelli and to join with all the other groups at
Sitka. The packet-boat Orel was at first also detailed
to take part in this expedition, but Navigator Talin, a
brazen character, wished to gainsay Baranov in

everything, and on this occasion he refused to proceed
as instructed. When Baranov discovered this he wrote,

> He (Talin) is angry. God knows why? I
> know no other reason than that I am an
> ordinary citizen of the Fatherland without
> service rank; that is what I think and
> assume about His Excellency's behavior.
> Fortunately, however, the whole matter was
> patched up and he was sent off to sea.[19]

Baranov left Kad'iak on May 25 on the galley Olga,
and when he arrived at Yakutat for an inspection he
found there an epidemic which already had claimed many
lives. The symptoms of the disease were as follows:
the victim felt nausea and constriction in the chest,
remained in agony from these symptoms for twenty-four
hours and then died. Even before leaving Kad'iak he had
learnt that a similar epidemic was raging in Kenai Bay,
and there had been many deaths there also.

In the fort at Yakutat he found affairs in disarray
with many disputes between the local people and the
manager. Baranov replaced him and restored order before
proceeding to Sitka. They rounded Cape Edgecumbe by a
hitherto unknown strait which they named Olga Strait
after their vessel.[20]

On July 7 Baranov arrived at the appointed place and
found there the Orel and a number of baidarkas. The
commandant of the new settlement, Medvednikov, when he
found the Kolosh well disposed towards him, had sent
back the main party of baidarkas as surplus to his
needs. Soon the brig Ekaterina arrived too. Baranov
called all the Kolosh toens together, spoke to them
gently, and gave them gifts, and they agreed to yield
him a site to build on. Baranov spent six days
examining other harbors and straits in the vicinity, but
finding no better place he agreed with Medvednikov's
choice. On the 15th they began to fell timber and
erect buildings.

On July 18 Baranov received news that the Aleuts had
halted in Khutsnov Strait to spend the night. They had

eaten many shellfish and during the next two hours more
than a hundred died in terrible convulsions. The sick-
ness began with nausea and dryness in the throat and
mouth, accompanied by cramps. The leaders of the party
considered inducing vomiting as the best remedy. They
had no medicaments and gave the sick dried gunpowder
and tobacco with soap. This remedy brought relief, but
the illness spread on the air and acted with equal
strength on those that remained.

During the stay in Sitka, Navigator Talin, as
Baranov says,

> avoided every meeting with me, and threatened
> his associates that if I came aboard he would
> have me lashed to the mast. That would not have
> scared me had it been necessary to board his
> ship, but there was no reason to, and I kept
> myself and him from sinning.[21]

The recalcitrant Talin offered none of his crewmen
to help in the building and Baranov, deciding that
Talin's presence was both unnecessary and pointless,
ordered the beaver pelts the Aleuts had caught to be
loaded onto the Orel, and then ordered the ship to go
straight to Kad'iak. Talin had made a prior agreement
with the former manager at Yakutat, Polomoshnoi, and
against his orders he put in there and took Polomoshoi
on board together with a load of furs that had been
stored there. When they got out into the open sea a
strong nor'wester was blowing, which forced the ship
towards Chugatsk Bay. She ran onto Sukli Island and was
wrecked. In this mishap five men were drowned, amongst
them Polomoshnoi. Up to 400 sea otter pelts were lost,
but the rest were salvaged and conveyed to Nuchek
Island. At current prices the loss in furs alone was
22,000 rubles, to say nothing of the vessel, with arms
and anchors.

Baranov hesitated: should he return to Kad'iak,
or spend the winter in the new fort? He remarked on his
quandary in a letter: "The situation on Kad'iak needs
my personal attention; there are many people there who

could make a mess of things, but not so many who can
put things right."

He decided to stay, however, and sent the <u>Ekaterina</u>
back to Kad'iak. Of the Aleut party some 50 baidarkas
remained at Sitka for fishing.

The winter of 1799 was a bad one. Violent storms
raged from October to January, almost without a break.
Then, through scarcity of food, scurvy broke out.
Baranov sought ways to keep his men healthy. He made
them keep on the move, aired out the cabins and made
some useful concoctions from roots and plants. These
seemed to succeed in helping the sick. But as soon as
the weather allowed he would send the Aleuts to sea to
shoot sea lions and hair seals, and to catch halibut
and codfish. This was the main way of restoring
peoples' health, and the consumption of fresh food
completely restored lost strength. Around February 20
they netted some herring and after that not only did
they have enough food but, to use Baranov's expression,
they "swam in a sea of plenty."

Describing the building of the new settlement,
Baranov wrote to the Company:

> of the buildings, we first erected a large
> balagan [shed], into which we unloaded all the
> materials from the ships and in which we
> stored the prepared food. Then we built a
> modest bathhouse, into which I moved in October,
> having had to exist up till then in a torn tent
> open to the elements; during the winter I
> suffered from the smoke and the damp from the
> leaks in the rotten roof, and unceasing bad
> weather until February. Next we built a two-
> story barrack building with two watchtowers
> on the corners. The building was eight
> sazhens long and four wide, with a cellar for
> storing supplies. [...] All this was completed
> with a very small labor force, because we were
> only 30 in all, of whom 20 were occupied in the
> construction, while ten were used as guards.[22]

Here he got to know English and American seafarers
who had come to trade with the natives. They traded
guns for fur, as well as powder and various other goods

including four pound caliber cannons, which Baranov saw
himself, and heard that an even bigger one had changed
hands. Before his very eyes in Sitka they bartered for
up to 2,000 sea otters:

> I more than once told them, Baranov writes,
> that such goods (guns and powder) ought not to
> be bartered to such barbarous people, because
> they often caused bloodshed amongst themselves
> and sometimes, as has happened, they even over-
> power vessels. Not only is it harmful and
> insulting for us, it disrupts good and peaceful
> relations between the Russian Court and the
> Republic of the United States. But they paid
> little heed to this; saying 'We're traders,
> we're after profits, there's no law against it!'[23]

Further on, he remarks, "When the Americans saw our
strongly built houses they said there was nothing they
could do there. They were amazed at our bravery and the
way we faced difficulties, and at our meager,
insufficient food, with only water to drink."[24]

Subsequently, the whole world learnt how the
foreigners trading in those straits envied the successes
of our hunters. They counted it quite normal to damage
everything everywhere, just so long as they got their
profits. Captain Vancouver had remarked on this back in
1793. He writes:

> And I am extremely concerned to be compelled
> to state here, that many of the traders from
> the civilized world have not only pursued a line
> of conduct, diametrically opposite to the true
> principles of justice in their commercial
> dealings, but have fomented discords, and stirred
> up contentions, between the different tribes, in
> order to increase the demand for these
> destructive engines [firearms].[25]

Towards winter Baranov became better acquainted
with the local population. The chief toen at Sitka,
Skautlelt, he especially feted and treated kindly. As
a sign of honor he gave him a bronze Russian coat of
arms and a testimonial dated March 25 1800, in which
Baranov attested that the land occupied by the Russians
for the fort was ceded by the toen and his tribe

voluntarily and for payment. The toen swore his
loyalty to Russia and in this document the Russians in
return promised to supply him with necessities and to
protect him from attack by warlike neighbors.[26]

Despite this apparently favorable treaty there was
almost constant discontent among the Kolosh. Those who
arrived from isolated regions taunted the Sitkans with
having become Russian vassals. They sneered at them,
vaunted their own freedom, and contrived to start
arguments and brazenly insult the Russians and Aleuts.
Baranov, on the Holy Easter holiday, wishing to entertain the toens, sent an interpreter into their settlement to invite them. All the Sitka toens appeared, but
the others robbed, beat up and drove off the envoy. On
the third day of the holiday, Baranov went to the
settlement in an armed rowboat with 22 men to punish
the arrogant offenders, and in his own words,

> to demonstrate to them our indifference, we
> stepped ashore unfrightened and walked in
> among their huts with only two guns, where
> more than 300 armed men had gathered. We
> cleaved a way through them towards the huts
> of the men who had slandered us. We were
> told that they were preparing to resist us;
> but after only two rounds of shot had been
> fired we found there only some old men, the
> rest had all fled.

The shots had been fired only to frighten and had
wounded no one. Baranov was pleased that the whole
thing had gone off without bloodshed, and he assembled
the elders, explained to them the baseness of their
deeds and asked the guilty to seek forgiveness. Then,
letting bygones be bygones, he made gifts to them and
the others, entertained them, and then sailed back.[27]

In treating with these peoples he could not and
dared not appear weak, nor could he use severe measures
in his dealings. He writes that: "our forces then
were very inadequate and need compelled us to seek
lenient methods." During the winter he invited many
toens into the fort, and, honoring them with ceremonial,

he let them amuse themselves with wild dances, the
usual passionate enjoyment of the savages on the Northwest Coast of America. Three times during such visits
savages were found with daggers hidden under their
capes -- they intended to strike down Baranov first,
as chief, and then to set about a wholesale extermin-
ation of the Russians.[28]

Baranov wintered in the new settlement, and when
ready to depart, he turned over the administration of
Kad'iak to the prikashchik Bakadarov. Navigator Talin
and some others hostile to Baranov took advantage of
Bakadarov's weak administration, and tried to forestall
Baranov's intentions, spreading discontent among the
Kad'iaks and inciting them to mutiny. Kuskov returned
from Nuchek in March of 1800 and largely succeeded in
quieting the discord. He assembled and sent off a
hunting party before Baranov's arrival. The turbulent
Talin, who had been shipwrecked on the Orel, refused
Baranov's request to turn over the log and other
necessary information, saying that Baranov, as a merchant, had no right to demand reports from him, reports
which he could only make to the Admiralty College.
Among the many unpleasant tidings Baranov received was
the news that Talin had encouraged the settlers to lay a
complaint against the manager, and he remarks in his
letters:

> What this slander consisted of I did not
> exactly find out, but it must have been full of
> reckless nonsense and stupidity and little else,
> for the Company and I have done everything for
> him that we could, and it was a matter of com-
> plete chance that losses and privations occurred
> which we too have to bear with patience.[29]

These investigations and slanders caused unrest, dis-
turbed all business and had people rushing about on
matters which Baranov had tried to stop at their very
inception.

Having calmed some minds and put matters straight,
he was about to set off for Kenai Bay to pacify the

savages there who were in revolt and who, according to
reports, had killed three Russians in the settlement on
the Iliamna River and were intent on wiping out everyone, including the Kad'iaks who were living there. But
this plot was discovered in time and the plotters, when
they had been seized and had confessed their guilt, were
transported to Kad'iak.[30]

Baranov was delayed from setting out by the
following circumstance: after a storm from the east
which continued for four days after May 26, various
articles and pieces of wreckage were found which made it
evident that the ship which had foundered was the
Phoenix -- this detained Baranov on Kad'iak. Try as he
might to find out about the wrecked ship, all his
inquiries both then and subsequently were fruitless,
and where, when and how the ship was wrecked remained a
mystery. From October of the preceding year articles
were thrown up on the shores of Kenai and Chugatsk Bays,
on various islands near Kad'iak and even on Ukamak
Island. Several worthy persons ascribed the loss to the
inexperience of Shields, whom they cursed, and called a
vagrant, and so forth. But Baranov did him justice by
recognizing his seamanship. One accident cannot and
should not destroy the good name of a man so eager to
pursue his duty. Shields had been valuable to the
Company, highly so, and his name deserves respect. Sea
disasters overtook Laperouse, Flinders and Freycinet, as
well as Shields.

Deprived of expected support from the cargo on the
Phoenix, with its stores and ammunition, Baranov was
short of many articles. He felt this even more because
he could send no transport vessel to Okhotsk. Only the
brig Ekaterina remained for communication between the
islands, apart from the little Olga, now almost worn out.
He supposed that the Company, having despatched the
Phoenix with her complement of people, goods and supplies, had no other vessel to send him that year, and on
this basis an enormous shortage of everything

threatened in the near future. In these circumstances
he resolved to send his deputy Potorochin by baidarka
to Unalashka to inform the manager Larionov of his
emergency, and to ask him for help.

Larionov had already (in December 1799) sent
baidarkas to Baranov, and, since he was a stockholder in
the Company, he advised that he was also participating
in the American ventures. Baranov gave him a detailed
description of the difficulties he was in and added
that, as far as he was concerned, the past ten years of
constant worry and care had undermined his health. He
asked to be relieved of his duties so that he could
set off for Okhotsk via Unalashka, or straight from
Kad'iak, adding that he was prepared to live there
taking no part in the trading, until the transport
arrived, and he could hand over affairs. Mentioning to
Larionov, in passing, some of the unpleasantnesses, he
wrote:

> More than anything I fear rows with unruly
> officials who consider affairs here from their
> own point of view. They are displeased at
> everything and make a fuss about everything
> and at everyone. They interrogate every
> arrival among the inhabitants and workers:
> Where and how do you live? Where do you work
> and what do you do? And they keep a written
> record of the answers.[31]

Further on he remarks,

> Do life, work and continued worry for the
> Company's good seem attractive when each step is
> accompanied by prejudiced judgments?[32] This is
> also part, in my opinion, of efforts for the
> general good and benefit of the Company and the
> Fatherland, which I undertook as my main object-
> ive when I began my duties as manager. I worked
> for them at the expense of my private gain and
> personal profit. Neither by word of mouth nor
> in writing, did I give any hopes, but I have
> proved and am proving by direct action what can
> be done. Devoting myself to this end, I have
> spared neither strength nor effort, and have
> often put my life in danger. Therefore, al-
> though there has been no request from you or my
> gentlemen colleagues, I would never neglect my

duty that lies before me, and the Administration
has always been able to depend on this. You may
see and judge for yourself from the present
profitable state of affairs that in a period
when my physical and spiritual strength is
ebbing, and with little help from the Company, I
have accomplished more than I claimed it would
and more than you could all have hoped to.[33]

In this extract it is impossible not to note the
language of truth and sincerity, and the lofty and noble
thoughts which Baranov expressed boldly and without any
self-adulation, which would have been alien to him.

The sea otter hunts during the year 1800 consisted
of a catch of 2,600 by the Sitka party and of 3,500
skins in the colonies as a whole.

Throughout the winter Baranov's enemies continued to
foist their convictions and troubles on the Kad'iak
people, so that many of the latter refused to go on a
hunting trip to Sitka, or to work for the Company in any
other way. Debilitating from the start, the consequences would have been extremely unfortunate, for
unpunished disobedience by the Kad'iaks could have
spread to other islands, and then the Russians, few in
number, would have lost everything they had achieved
after so much effort and time in various places in
America, and might themselves have become victims of
this weakening. Baranov foresaw all this and took wise
and decisive measures to put down the mutiny. He sent
armed detachments to all settlements and demanded hostages of all the more suspect toens who were inclined to
rebellion. This bold act forestalled the harmful plot
and the natives of Kad'iak remained obedient,[34] or as
Baranov himself puts it:

They agreed once more to live as they had
formerly and to join the expeditions: and all
this, of course, without the least bloodshed on
either side and no punishment, not even a lenient
fine was levied on the guilty because of their
frank confession of guilt and their repentance.[35]

CHAPTER IV

On April 24, 1801, the first United States trading
ship, the _Enterprise_, arrived in Kad'iak from New York.
Her Captain, James Scott, brought Baranov a message from
the manager at Sitka, and proposed that he exchange part
of his cargo for furs. Baranov had to accept this proposal because of pressing needs, but it caused him great
difficulties since under the trading rules at that time
all pelts had to be divided between the Company and the
hunters; consequently the exchange with foreigners for
general wares broke these conditions. On the other
hand the complete lack of goods throughout the colonies,
for clothing and for paying the Russian employees, and
for paying Aleuts for hunting, forced a change in the
previous system. Necessity alters laws. The loss of
the _Phoenix_ had removed the possibility of supplies
from Okhotsk, and there was no news of the party sent
to Unalashka for supplies in July of the previous year.
In this extremity Baranov decided to trade with the
foreigners, but as the Captain offered low prices for
pelts, only 2,000 black and red fox furs were exchanged.
From these visitors Baranov learnt of the continuing war
all over Europe; they frightened him with tales that
Spain, acting in concert with France, intended to arm
frigates and send them to our colonies. If this
happened, for want of official information he might
accept the enemies as allies and vice-versa. Thus
Baranov was informed by his deputy Larionov, whom he
asked to forward him news as it came from Russia.

In May, as the Americans were leaving, Potorochin
arrived from Unalashka by baidarka, having left there
on September 29. Storms had delayed his journey all
through the winter. This reveals how unreliable and

dangerous was communication between the islands in small leather craft and how precious and irreplaceable was the time lost in this way. They managed to bring a few supplies in the baidarkas, and confirmation of the articles washed ashore from the Phoenix, which they had found all along the coast from Unalashka to Alaska.

In the summer of 1801 Baranov received news dated May 9 from Malakhov at the Konstantinovsk fort: two of the former rebels had fled, and reaching the Copper River had raised the local people and set out to one of the sounds of Chugatsk Bay where they were recruiting new members from the local tribes, intending to attack the fort. Baranov set off at once on the galley Olga, first to Kenai Bay, and then to the Konstantinovsk fort where he discovered the rebels scattered already by their own inner discord, and he returned to Kad'iak on September 28. The brig Ekaterina delivered from Sitka all the pelts caught by Kuskov's party and gained by barter at the settlement in all, nearly 5,000 skins. Kuskov, who had returned on the same vessel, reported that with his party, he had gone round Sitka Island and found a great many sea otter on the shores: he had everywhere made the Koloshes gifts, and they had not hindered the hunting.

In April of the following year (1802) Baranov again sent Kuskov off with a party of Aleuts on the same journey. In May the Titular Councilor Banner arrived by baidarka from Unalashka. He had just entered the Company's service,[36] and had been sent to the colonies by Larionov to get practice and experience from Baranov in administration and organization, so that he might subsequently replace him when he left America. Together with this, news was received of the Company coming under Imperial patronage with a grant of privileges, of Baranov's inclusion among the stockholders, and further, of the enthronement of Emperor Alexander. Baranov was also handed an Imperial decoration from the late Emperor Paul, the gold medal and band of Vladimir, given for

services rendered. He this regarded as a day of
triumph, and describes it thus:

> In the barracks they sang the "hours" and
> prayers, and then the Imperial parchment was
> read, also the acts enforcing privileges, etc.
> to general rejoicing, and then I placed round
> my aging neck my Monarch's sign of excellence
> – about which no one knew in advance. In my
> sincere enthusiasm at this gift from the
> Monarch I could only express my spiritual
> gratitude by a weak imitation of such
> generosity. In the school here I subscribed
> 1,000 rubles for Russian orphans and children
> of the islanders. For this feast-day we
> slaughtered one of the elderly yamans [sheep].

What luxury!!

On June 21 Baranov sent the vessel Ekaterina to
Yakutat and Sitka, with reinforcements, and at the same
time he sent Banner to Unalashka to fetch needed
supplies and goods. In July Banner left Kad'iak on the
galley Olga under Kashevarov's command. Baranov wrote
to Larionov that he himself wished to set out for Sitka
but was detained only by fear of attack by hostile
European powers. At that time the storehouses were full
of rich goods which he intended to hide in the interior
of the island. He writes:

> It is true, if strong enemy forces arrive,
> it would be wise to save the furs, but at least
> as long as we have strength and with God's help
> we think of ways of defending ourselves and pre-
> serving them, it is better that they should be
> here in front of us. We are building a battery
> in one narrow place; but we have few large guns
> and not one large caliber shell.

On the 24th of the same month the English ship
Unicorn arrived at Kad'iak. Her Captain, Barber,
delivered three Russians, two Aleuts and 18 Kad'iak
women who had been rescued from the Kolosh, after the
latter had destroyed the fort on Sitka. Baranov was
then on a journey to Afognak and some of the other
islands, but when he received this news he quickly
returned.

Those who witnessed these unfortunate and terrible

events related that a great force of Kolosh had
attacked the fort at mid-day; they had given the
Russians an agonising death: they had plundered the sea
otter pelts in the storehouses and had reduced the
settlement and a boat which was under construction to
ashes.

Barber did not put the former prisoners ashore, but
displayed 20 cannon and armed his men. He informed
Baranov that although he belonged to a nation at war
with Russia he had out of humanity ransomed these people
from the hands of savages, clothed and fed them. He had
had to break off his trading operations to bring them
to Baranov. In recompense for all this, he demanded
50,000 rubles in cash or in furs at a price which he
would determine. But Baranov discovered that on the
contrary, Barber had not only paid no ransom for them,
but according to the evidence of the prisoners, he had
seized the ringleaders responsible for the destruction--
the toens Skautlelt and his nephew Kotleian--had clapped
them in irons and threatened to hang them from the yard
arm. In this way the sympathetic Barber forced them to
cede him many of the sea otter pelts plundered from the
settlement and his expenses had merely been to clothe
and feed the prisoners during less than a month's
journey.

The incompatibility of such demands with obligations,
and the warlike threats put Baranov in a tight corner.
Yet, unafraid, he steadfastly rejected the Briton's
shameless demands and took what defensive measures his
strength allowed to repulse any attack. Meanwhile he
and Barber continued their talks, and finally agreed on
a ransom of 10,000 rubles worth of furs. When these
were delivered to the Captain, with a receipt, he
released the prisoners.

The vessel Ekaterina arrived in Kad'iak on September
5 from Yakutat, where Kuskov had been with the hunting
party. He had repulsed an attack by the Kolosh on the
way to Sitka, and had reached a point near Sitka when

he learnt that the Kolosh intended to destroy the
settlement there. He halted and sent ahead several
baidarkas to warn the fort, but when his Aleuts arrived
in the night they found that the new settlement had been
plundered, burnt, and left empty. They hurried back to
Kuskov with this sorry news, and then they all returned
to Yakutat together. Several days later they were
joined there by Urbanov, the leader of another expedition. He and some Aleuts had been sent from Sitka to
hunt and they had thereby survived the destruction of
the fort.[37]

Their arrival in Kad'iak in no way eased Baranov's
desperate position. He had earlier been tormented by
not knowing the fate of the expeditions sent from Sitka
and Kad'iak, but in all this he thanked God and considered it especially fortunate that the settlement at
Yakutat had remained intact, and that his assistant
Kuskov and his party had returned without loss --
unsuccessfully, but safely.

Baranov was extremely depressed by the loss of the
settlement at Sitka. It was a harrowing experience for
him; he realized that this misfortune had greatly
hampered his original plan to occupy places beyond Sitka.
Weighing the impact of the loss, he resolved firmly to
reoccupy the settlements, at the first opportunity. He
desired to preserve the Nation's fame in the eyes of the
foreign traders, to keep the trust placed in him by the
Government and the Company, and, by expanding trade and
hunting, to make them yield profits, and thus render new
service to the Fatherland.

Evils and misfortunes incline people to know more of
God's grace than do uninterrupted happiness and peace.
Through their troubled understanding they can feel and
see a Higher Force, unexpectedly leading them out of the
abyss of evil, where human reasoning alone would have
had them perish. Having passed through a school of
suffering, they learn to recognise their mistakes and

try to act more carefully and to build on firmer found-
ations.

Driven by grief at these recent disasters, Baranov
was overjoyed by the arrival of ships: from Unalashka
came the Olga with Banner, while from Okhotsk came the
brig Aleksandr under Navigator Petrov on September 13,
and on November 1 the brig Elisaveta, under Lieutenant
N. A. Khvostov. On these last two ships came more than
120 promyshlenniks and a most inadequate cargo of goods
and supplies.

The Company directors gave just honor and respect to
Baranov by appointing him Chief Manager of the colonies
in America, in charge of Unalashka and the other districts, authorizing him to establish offices in them,
to combine all Company possessions and to put everything
on the same footing. Thus all the previously issued
furs should go to the Company at a uniform rate and be
paid for in money. This new system was more profitable
to the Company than to the promyshlenniks and met with
stiff opposition. This cost Baranov much time and worry
and several years correspondence with the Directors.

I will not describe these exhausting arguments and
counter-arguments - they are not of particular interest.
Their consequences can be seen in the general contracts
made with the promyshlenniks, from which, by comparing
earlier and later confirmations by the Main Office of
Baranov's projects, it can be seen how the conditions
and relations between the Company and the promyshlenniks
had changed.

Then he received a copy of a document, the original
of which had been despatched on the Phoenix. From this
he learnt that the Archimandrite Ioasaf, newly confirmed
as Bishop, had been returning to Kad'iak with his
retinue and a wealth of church vestments and utensils.
Ninety passengers and a significant cargo of goods had
fallen victim to the stormy seas.

In April, 1803, Baranov, on assuming the administration of all the colonies, sent Banner on the galley

Olga to Unalashka with written instructions for the
administrator there. He was to send to Kad'iak the ship
Petr i Pavel with men and whatever goods and supplies
were available in the storehouses there. He was to
select the best fur seals and temporarily suspend their
unprofitable hunting on Paul and George Islands; as they
had not been shipped out, a stock of 800,000 pelts had
built up, and through lack of warehouses to protect
them from damp and other influences, they had spoiled.
Baranov also asked that the hunters agree to the new
conditions sent by the Main Office, and gave other minor
instructions, for Banner and the Unalashka manager to
fulfill.

In June Khvostov set out for Okhotsk on the brig
Elisaveta with a very valuable cargo; there were more
than 17,000 sea otter pelts, and with all other furs
this cargo was valued at 1,200,000 rubles.

Baranov set out for Yakutat in the galley Olga.
There he found both his vessels and Kuskov, who had
returned with a party of Aleuts and a meager catch of
sea otters. Baranov then planned to proceed to Sitka,
reoccupy the lost site, and show the Kolosh that whereas
during the alliance the Russians had been their true
friends, they would now find that because of their, the
Kolosh', treachery and theft the Russians could be
merciless avengers. However, he respected Kuskov's
sensible advice that in this late season the baidarkas
might founder in a storm and an unsuccessful expedition
could only encourage the Kolosh. Thus the journey to
Sitka was postponed. Meantime, in order to strengthen
their fleet, instructions were given to build two small
sailing boats at Yakutat. Kuskov and shipwrights were
placed in charge of this, while Baranov himself returned
to Kad'iak on October 14. Here he found the American
ship O'Cain under Captain O'Cain, who two years earlier
had been boatswain on the Enterprise, and exchanged a
goods cargo for 10,000 rubles. O'Cain suggested that he
be supplied with Aleuts and baidarkas so he could hunt

sea otters off the California coast and then return to
Kad'iak where the whole catch would be divided. The
trouble Baranov now faced as to sea otter hunting with
his own forces had deprived him of the prospect of a
profitable haul; for along the coast around Sitka every
sea otter had to be fought for with fierce enemies until
permanent settlements could be established there with
strong mutual support. Therefore he decided, when he
had received from O'Cain most of the goods to maintain
the party, to give him 20 baidarkas under the supervision of his trusted and sensible employee Shvetsov,
whom he instructed to inspect all the places on the
coast where they should put in. In this way Baranov
hoped to receive reliable information about places
where sea otters were still to be found. He also wished
to acquaint himself with the inhabitants of California,
at that period known only through confused tales of
foreigners. He wished to know what products originated
there and, finally, what measures the Americans were
taking for trading with the Californians and the savages
inhabiting the Northwest Coast of America. He also
wanted information on whether, what, and how much they
paid them for local produce, and so forth.

On October 26 they set sail from Kad'iak, called at
the port of San Diego and thence went to San Quentin
Bay where they hunted sea otter until March 1. When the
pelt take reached 1,100, as arranged they returned to
Kad'iak. Shvetsov informed Baranov of the produce of
those places they had visited and that O'Cain had used
his own goods in San Diego and San Quentin to barter for
furs from the missionaries and soldiers. In this way he
had gained up to 700 sea otter pelts at three to four
piasters a pelt.

On March 23 1804, Navigator Bubnov arrived by
baidarka from Unalashka. He had been sent from Okhotsk
to Kad'iak in the previous year on the transport ship
Dimitrii, but the ship had been wrecked near Umnak
Island. However, all the cargo, crew, and passengers

had been saved. With Bubnov's arrival Baranov learned
that thanks to the recommendation of the Main Office of
the Company, for services rendered and duties performed,
the Emperor had most graciously conferred upon him the
rank of Collegiate Assessor.

Then, shedding tears of gratitude for the
beneficence of the Monarch, who appreciated these services in such far off parts, he cried with fervor, "I
have been rewarded, but Sitka is lost! No! I cannot
live! I shall go--and I shall either die or make it
another of the territories of my most August Patron!"

CHAPTER V

On April 2 a party of Aleuts in 300 baidarkas under
Dem'ianenkov was sent off, and the Manager himself with
the vessels Ekaterina and Aleksandr left Kad'iak on
April 4 and arrived in Yakutat on May 25. Here he
found that as he had instructed, the two sailing vessels
had been completed under Kuskov's direction; he named
them the Ermak and the Rostislav.

Sending the ships Ekaterina and Aleksandr to Sitka
and a party under protection of the sailing boat
Rostislav, Baranov himself left Yakutat on the Ermak on
August 25 and joined the party in Cross Sound (Icy
Strait) on August 26. Both boats and the baidarkas
entered the sound early in the morning. Suddenly an
extraordinarily thick fog, which usually remains there
all year round, hid them from the shore and the wall of
ice at the entrance to the sound. It was even
impossible to see from vessel to vessel or to the surrounding baidarkas. At that moment, to increase the
danger, the current from the sea into the sound strengthened and its force carried the Ermak off into the ice
and between perilous cliffs and rock-faces, whither, as
Baranov had noted, even the bravest Kolosh dared not
take their boats. They could then find no single means
of salvation; the wind had dropped and the sails were
useless; the tow-lines were powerless to combat the
current in the sound and it was too deep to anchor.
Nothing remained but to seek the mercy of Almighty
Providence. In this peril the tide began to ebb, taking
them back with the same force through the same dangers.
Baranov, who knew how to calculate speed by certain
comparisons, probably could not find one adequate, as
witness his strange expression, "Like going into the

44

mouth of Hell! Among icebergs which were like mountains
and touched the yards." It seemed that Fate stared
them in the face and Death surrounded them on all sides.
Between the huge walls of ice the current produced
whirlpools where the vessels twirled together with the
floating pack-ice, pressed on each side by this piece or
that. Here they had to use every possible effort to
push themselves away with poles to escape being crushed.
But what good is man's puny strength against the mighty
forces of nature? Only God's inscrutable grace can
bring salvation. After a torturing twelve hours in this
mortal danger, eventually, to their great joy, they
escaped the ice and anchored in a small port where the
Rostislav and the hunting party had arrived after under-
going the same dangers as the Ermak. The Ermak had lost
her dinghy in the ice, the Rostislav her tiller, and the
hunting party a three-seater baidarka.

When they had lain in the bay for three days because of contrary winds in the sound, the bold Baranov
decided once again to attempt that same passage through
which no sailing vessel had yet ventured to pass. As
evidence of this are the words of Langsdorf who, travelling through this channel by baidarka with the experienced American seafarer D'Wolf, remarks that the stream
was so rapid, that it was like going down a waterfall.
The distance from shore to shore is not more than 150
toises; the length of the strait some 200 paces, and the
fall of the water was, according to their calculations,
up to 5 feet. Mr. D'Wolf assured him that he had never
anywhere seen such a rush of water, and he therefore
concluded that those Russian seafarers who had dared to
pass through it must be extremely skilful and brave.[38]

In good weather and with a following current both
ships and the baidarkas passed round or through great
masses of ice and towards evening they entered the broad
open Khutsnov Strait (Chatham Strait) and from there
entered Chil'khat Sound (Lynn Canal). On the way to the
bay of sea otters they passed some Kolosh villages:

Kaknaut, Koukontan, Akku, Taku, Tsultana, Stakhin, Kek
and Kuiu. The party of Aleuts hunted sea otters freely
and killed up to 1,500 of all sorts. Whenever the
people in the settlements caught sight of the Russians
they would run away in fear. They passed by all these
settlements except the last two, the inhabitants of
which had wiped out Urbanov's expedition. As punishment for this they burned all the buildings. From there
the vessels rounded Sitka Island and on September 8
arrived safely at Krestov Harbor, where the party of
Aleuts also arrived four days later. Here Baranov found
the following vessels waiting for him: the Ekaterina,
the Aleksandr, and the ship Neva, which had sailed round
the world.

Captain-Lieutenant Lisianskii of the Neva had
arrived in Kad'iak on July 1. There received a communication from Baranov explaining the state of affairs
in America and he hastened to co-operate with him in
regaining the lost territories. Leaving Kad'iak on
August 3 he reached Sitka after five days and there
waited for Baranov. Baranov asked Captain Lisianskii to
help him to persuade the Kolosh to return the places
they had taken from the Russians, and if they refused,
to help him compel them by force of arms. They conferred, and deciding on a course of action, on the 17th
left Krestov Harbor with all the ships, and the party of
Aleuts. Towards evening they stood at anchor off the
Sitka settlement, opposite the Kekur, (a high rock)
where, however, they found all the huts empty. The inhabitants had all withdrawn to the fort they had built
on the cape near the river further along the Bay. On
the 18th the toen Kotleian with a small group of people
approached the fort for a parley. When he was asked to
provide hostages he demanded to be given the same number
of Russians and Aleuts. As he showed no inclination to
make peace he was ordered to withdraw. In order to
clear the surrounding shore they fired several balls to
see if anyone was waiting in ambush for them to dis-

embark from the vessels. After this, Baranov landed and
occupied the high and steep Kekur, raised the flag as a
sign of the authority of the Russian state, and pro-
claimed it once again Novo-Arkhangel'sk fort. On the
Kekur they sited and manned the cannon, and the Aleuts
occupied all the surrounding countryside. Then a Kolosh
baidara was sighted going from the sea to the fort.
Lieutenant Arbuzov was detailed by Captain Lisianskii to
chase it. When they were attacked the Kolosh put up a
desperate defence, firing from rifles. The gunpowder in
the baidara soon blew up and most of the Kolosh were
drowned, only six being saved; of these, two of the
gravely injured soon died and the others were captured
and taken aboard the Neva.

By early evening a peace emissary from the Kolosh
arrived at our fort. He was told that the toens themselves should come for talks. Next day the same emissary arrived bringing one hostage, but they sent him
away again with the same answer. Soon after, some 60
Kolosh appeared on the shore. Some of them remained
halfway to the fort, and the others, wearing armor and
carrying rifles and spears came up to the fort on the
Kekur - among them being the toens. Baranov proposed to
them that everything past should be forgotten; he
demanded only the return of the remaining Aleut
prisoners, and that, in order to secure the Russians'
presence there, they should give hostages and also
should abandon their own fort and go farther off, beyond
the places we occupied. The talks lasted about two
hours, but the Kolosh refused these very moderate terms
and, shouting three times, "Oo! Oo! Oo!," they went
away.

On the 20th all our vessels approached the enemy
fort as far as the water depth would allow. They
anchored and opened fire on the fort. The Kolosh
answered from all sides with several cannonades.
According to Baranov, the Kolosh fort was made of very
thick tree trunks laid two or more together, then dug-

outs were set in a shallow depression in the ground.
Because of this, and the distance involved, our gunfire
did the enemy no harm. Captain Lisianskii sent an
armed landing-party under Lieutenants Arbuzov and
Povalishin. When the men landed they began to converge
on the fort from various directions. Baranov hurried to
send a support party with two field-pieces to join
forces with Arbuzov. With four cannon they approached
the fort from the right, keeping up an incessant fire on
it. Baranov remarks: "the very thickness of the wood
of the fort made it hard to do it any significant damage, while we were exposed from all sides and, in
addition, dusk was falling." This decided them to take
the fort by storm, but the Kolosh gathered all their
forces together and opened a heavy fire from their fort.
At that very moment when the fort should have been
smashed and set on fire, Baranov was wounded in the
right arm by a ricochet and Lieutenant Povalishin was
also wounded. Some of the promyshlenniks and Aleuts
who were not used to battle took flight. Then it was
decided to retreat in good order and withdraw to the
ships.

In this foray three sailors, three promyshlenniks
and four Aleuts were killed and two sailors, nine promyshlenniks and six Aleuts wounded: in all there were 10
dead and 24 wounded, amongst these latter the two
officers. Shortly after this, Baranov called before him
one of the warlike Aleut toens, Nankok (well known among
visitors to Sitka) and reproached him for cowardice and
having fled.

Nankok, wishing to justify himself, said, "I am
sorry, Aleksandr Andreevich, but I will not go forward."

Baranov answered jokingly, "I know that you will not
go forward, but at least do not run to the rear and so
set an example to your followers!"

On the 21st Baranov, in pain from his wound, was in
no shape for military operations, and he therefore
begged Captain Lisianskii to take complete command and

to act as he should see fit.[39] Lisianskii ordered the
ships to keep up heavy cannon fire on the fort. This
eventually produced the desired result – the Kolosh
asked for a parley, and talks concerning the sending of
hostages and the release of the prisoners opened.

On the 22nd the Kolosh hung out a white flag on the
fort and delivered ten hostages on board the Neva.

On the 23rd some prisoners were released to the ship
– one Aleut, two Kad'iak women, and, on the following
day, one more Kad'iak woman.

On the 26th, seeing no activity in the fort,
Lisianskii sent a landing party, who found that it had
been deserted. During the night the Kolosh had fled
through the hills to Khutsnov Strait, leaving behind
three old women. Near the fort 30 bodies were counted,
and inside, those of five children killed by the Kolosh
before they fled. The spoils for the victors were three
cast iron falconets and several rifles, and on the
beach, 30 large boats. Next day the Kolosh fort was
demolished and set on fire. The old women who had been
discovered in the fort were in accordance with their own
wishes given a boat in which to go and seek their fellow
tribesmen.

After driving off the Kolosh, the ships sailed back
to the Novo-Arkhangel'sk fort and lay at anchor there.

Yet they did not know for sure where the Kolosh had
gone. They assumed, as said above, that they had all
fled to the hills, but on the 25th and 26th eight Aleuts
were found murdered near the bay. They then realised
that the Kolosh were sitting it out in the woods,
waiting for a chance to surprise the Aleuts as they went
fishing, so they took the necessary precautions to avoid
this.

The first building put up near the site of the fort
was one needed for storage. Almost a thousand trees
were felled to make a stockade, and a small plank cabin
was built for the Manager. A belltower and watchtower

were built with surrounds of sharpened spikes; pro-
tecting the fort from hostile onslaughts by the Kolosh.

Baranov kept by him in the new settlement all the
ships and baidarkas except the Rostislav, sent to
Kad'iak with news. On November 10 the Neva also set out
to winter there. In spring, after she had taken on
board all furs, she was to call in again at Sitka with
messages from the Main Office for Baranov and then
follow her prescribed course to Canton.

On board the Neva, when she left, were the four
Kolosh captured by Lieutenant Arbuzov when their baidara
exploded. Baranov wrote to the Kad'iak office: "They
must be dispersed amongst the various artels and given
the same tasks as the Aleut workers; if they misbehave,
they are to be punished, but they must be kept clothed
and shod." About victualling the complement of the Neva
he wrote Banner asking him to let them have mainly fowl
and fish, and to hold back as many cattle as possible,
for breeding, so that an important part of the economy
would not fail.

All winter the Kolosh toens never appeared at the
fort, though from time to time they sent small scouting
bands to spy on the Russians, who meantime worked
zealously. The Aleuts fished all the time.

On June 10 1805, the Neva arrived from Kad'iak.
Captain-Lieutenant Lisianskii, when he saw the solid
buildings and the many articles of husbandry, was
amazed at Baranov's unceasing efforts and unexpected
successes. Soon afterwards there arrived toen Saiginakh,
Kotleian's brother, who was entertained in a kindly
fashion by Baranov in the fort.

The Neva was loaded with 3,000 beavers, 150,000
seals and many other goods to the sum, according to
prices then current in the colonies, of around 450,000
rubles. With this valuable cargo Captain Lisianskii
left Sitka on August 20, and sailed direct to Canton.

At Baranov's suggestion he took with him from
Kad'iak three creole boys, who knew how to read and

write. He was to deliver them to St. Petersburg for
further education.[40]

On the 26th the brig _Maria_ under Lieutenant Mashin
arrived from Kamchatka bearing the plenipotentiary of
the Company, Actual Chamberlain N. P. Rezanov, who had
left the vessel _Nadezhda_ on the return journey from his
ambassadorship in Japan. With him as passengers were
Lieutenants Khvostov and Davydov and the naturalist
Langsdorf. On the way Rezanov had called in at Kad'iak
and inspected the affairs of the Company's Office there.
When he had acquainted himself with the present extent
of progress, he realized that there was still much to be
done to bring the colony into the condition the State
would wish to see it.

Baranov reported to him upon all areas of activity,
and as a result Rezanov sought to give the colonies a
new form. As of September 1 he required a Council, to
establish the area so that:

> the profits extracted by the Company should be
> firmly guaranteed, the cultivating and hus-
> bandry branches should flourish and crafts and
> manufactures should ease the need of the in-
> habitants: trading should be based on standard
> rules of conduct; the administration and the law
> should guarantee safety of person as well as
> property; sea travel with adequate vessels and
> men should be guaranteed; military forces, in
> good order and discipline, should offer every-
> one necessary protection from enemies; the
> duties of the inhabitants should be equal to
> their capabilities; and humanity should be
> respected to the full.

In reply to this Baranov laid before him many
specific and general failings which needed correction.
Considering these, Rezanov drew up rules for administering the colonies under 17 headings and forwarded
them to Baranov on September 9, beginning thus:

> The closer my acquaintance with the present
> position of the Russian-American Company; its
> territories in the New World; the hunting,
> trading, navigation and husbandry branches; the
> fortifications, and so forth; the more failings
> I discover. Lack of possibilities and of

structure exist in the very organization of its
trading society. I foresee that because of its
expanding institutions, it should be trans-
formed completely in accordance with ventures
undertaken, and thus provide a firm basis for
all its branches of activity. Otherwise everything could fail at once. A single unfortunate
combination of circumstances could upset everything and ruin the Company's credit. These
changes should be made in the Company statute,
with approval of the authorities, in order to
establish an irrevocable law which will unite
this rambling colossus forever and set up
definite development plans with harsh punish-
ments for each departure from the given rules.

In the first three paragraphs of this regulation he
focussed on reforming the Company itself, and establish-
ing its various administrative areas. In the fourth
paragraph, on hunting, he remarks:

men who enter the Company's service for hunting
are used instead for building, fortification,
navigation and defence. Less than 400 people
make up our total strength in America, hold
down the natives, and at the same time preserve
this whole coast, and in reward for this they
receive a half share of animals caught. The
number of people in the industry is too small
for efficiency but to increase the number on
the existing basis would be unprofitable both
for them and the Company, especially if the
returns from hunting should diminish. It is
therefore necessary to persuade people to
accept payment in cash, leaving all the industry
calculations to the company alone.

Rezanov then outlined special proposals giving a
scale of the staff required in all the different
locations and the appropriate salary schedules. He
further emphasized the need to introduce manufacturing
and handicrafts, schools and charitable institutions.
He also advised that experiments be conducted in cultivation, that younger boys should be sent to the capital
for education and training in trades, the arts, and so
on. Commending these measures to Baranov he says:

indeed all private undertakings must spring
from these beginnings, and by leading people
at a quiet, true pace to enlightenment, we

must subtly lead them to forms of behavior
suited best to their respective locations.

And finally, addressing Baranov, he says,

because I know your noble nature I will now
open a wider field for your activity with
complete confidence that you as an eager and
enthusiastic son of the Fatherland will use
it to the best advantage. I am sure that
from now on all your reports will draw
greater recognition from our fellow countrymen, and thousands of voices will unite in
your just praise. There can be no doubt
that you will come even to the notice of his
Imperial Majesty.

If Rezanov had arrived perhaps five, or even two
years earlier, in a period which had been miserable for
Baranov, when he had not received reinforcements on the
Phoenix, when he had neither sufficient men, nor ship
stores, nor goods, nor necessities; or at the time when
he had just lost the Sitka settlement, when he was
pressed by circumstances and threatened by new misfortunes and internal troubles; then he would have been
inclined more to proposals that were arranged on a
smaller scale. But now Rezanov found the lost territory already won back, ship commanders with skill and
experience, and, by comparison with former times, an
adequate population. Expectations of sea otter yields,
and the possibility of obtaining everything needed by
exchange or purchase from foreigners, made it seem to
him very convenient to place the colonies on a well-
based foundation; to set up handicrafts, manufacturing
and so forth, as it were with a stroke of the pen.

Studying Baranov's circumstances and undertakings
from the very beginning, it becomes clear that all these
proposals were never possible in his administration.
He had to struggle with cold and hunger, needs of every
kind, and with both internal and external foes. He well
knew that the first stages in progressing from savagery
to civilisation were handicraft and craftsmanship; but
the occupations could only be given to literate people,

which he did not have. I repeat that he knew that
education and enlightenment should derive from enlightened pastors and teachers; as witness to this we
have his first letter to Shelikhov, written when he
arrived in the Aleutian Islands, but his wishes were
thwarted. When the Archimandrite left for Okhotsk, the
religious mission, bereft of senior direction, made not
a step forward in its parish. Rezanov himself notes
this, saying, "the religious mission, although it bap-
tised many Americans, did not achieve much, for they all
remained in the same stage of ignorance."

With the arrival of two vessels from Okhotsk the
number of officials and workers had increased signific-
antly. But Baranov had neither luxury articles to
satisfy their needs, nor even the basic necessities. In
the past, often and for long periods, Baranov and his
men had lived off the crude local food, without even
thinking of bread, but now the new people, encouraged by
His Excellency's patronage and good disposition began to
press their various needs. And, as in fact they needed
almost everything, at Baranov's suggestion it was
decided to trade and buy D'Wolf's ship with all its
cargo. On September 28 it was agreed that the price
should be 68,000 piasters. This sum broke down into
31,250 piasters worth of furs and the remainder was
transferred as exchange at the Main Office in St.
Petersburg. Khvostov was made captain of the Juno and
Davydov his second in command.

As part of the purchase price of the Juno, D'Wolf
was also given two boats, the Ermak outright, and the
Rostislav for a limited period. On the first he sent
his crew and supplies off to the Sandwich Islands, and
on the other he himself went to the port of Okhotsk,
from whence he intended to journey to St. Petersburg.

On his arrival in Sitka, Rezanov intended to order
two vessels built, but now that the Juno had been purchased, only a cutter was needed. Two craftsmen were
employed in building it: Koriukin, who had been round

the world on the <u>Neva</u>, and Popov, who had come via
Okhotsk.

Rezanov understood well how important and taxing
were Baranov's wide ranging responsibilities, how
limited and hard pressed he was for means and materials
and how he suffered from lack of manpower. He therefore considered it necessary and just to reward those
under him for their efforts and to encourage them in the
future. At Baranov's recommendation (by virtue of the
authority vested in Rezanov) a gold medal on a Vladimir
ribbon was awarded to Kuskov; and silver medals to
Malakhov, Shvetsov, Bakadarov and Eremin.

In spite of the foodstuffs bought from D'Wolf, the
need for more increased daily. At Baranov's request
Rezanov agreed to send Khvostov on the <u>Juno</u> to Kad'iak
to bring back iukola, whalemeat and blubber. On October
4 Khvostov set out to sea[41] and returned on November 13
with iukola and other goods and thus satisfied the
promyshlenniks' and Aleuts' need for provisions.

CHAPTER VI

Khvostov brought sorrowful news for Baranov from
Kad'iak: The brig Elisaveta, which had set out for
Kad'iak under the command of Lieutenant Sukin had been
wrecked and most of her cargo lost. That which had been
salvaged was damaged by the salt water. Also six baidaras sent from the hunting parties with cargoes of fur
had foundered during a storm, and more than 200 of the
Aleuts sent from Sitka, under the command of
Dem'ianenkov, had perished at sea. Finally, as if that
were not enough, the fort at Yakutat with its garrison
and inhabitants had been wiped out by the Kolosh.[42]

The weight of all these misfortunes falling suddenly
upon Baranov, bent, but did not crush him. These disasters grieved him all the more since they had happened
during a visit by an important and dear guest whom he
had wished only to please with good tidings and news of
success. Rezanov, an enlightened and noble spirit, com-
forted the old man, suggesting new ways and means to
retrieve the losses, or at least in some way to lighten
them, and promised to aid in any way he could.

The loss of the fort and men at Yakutat, so touching
and important for Baranov, is worth description, however
pitiful and grievous.

We have already seen that the party of Aleuts under
Dem'ianenkov, after wintering in Sitka, had set out for
Kad'iak. En route they learnt that the Yakutat settlement had been destroyed by the Kolosh who were also
trying to ambush and kill them as they travelled. Their
experienced leader, although he could not quite believe
this news, could not refute it either, and therefore
gave orders to travel only at night or in overcast
weather, and to stay put during the day.

56

The crossing from the hamlet Akoi to Yakutat is a
distance of about 60 versts; the party planned their
journey so that they could arrive at night and get news
of the settlement. Such a distance would require at
least ten hours of concentrated rowing. They arrived
off the settlement late at night, and to their great
sorrow learned the truth of the rumors they had heard.
Everything was in ruins. Constantly fearing attack by
the Kolosh, they left shore as quickly as they could.
The weak and exhausted Aleuts dared not land where the
enemy waited for them, nor could they continue to row
for any length of time; many were weak from exertion.
Then Dem'ianenkov called all the baidarkas together and
asked the Aleutians to choose: either they went ashore
regardless, or they cast themselves on God's mercy and
made straight for Nuchek. The majority decided to make
for Kaiak Island about 200 miles distant. But the exhausted, about 30 baidarkas in all, refused, saying they
could not go on. They decided to make for the shore and
captivity and slavery or torture and death at the hands
of the Kolosh. Bitter though this separation was, they
had no strength to go on rowing. It must be said that
the shore between Yakutat and Chugatsk Bay is rocky and
steep, in places inaccessible. Because of the shallows
there is no easy access, even for rowing boats, in
stormy weather. God and the Fates had decreed that
those who thought they were going to certain death
should be saved. They reached the shore exhausted, but
rested unharmed by the Kolosh, and then continued their
journey. In the meanwhile a terrible storm had arisen,
fatal for their comrades. When the storm dropped and
the remaining group sailed further, they found baidarkas
and the disfigured bodies of their brothers and relatives washed up on the shore. They reached Nuchek, and
then Kad'iak, in safety. There they discovered that all
of those who had been strong enough to set out for Kaiak
had perished on the stormy sea.
Now about Yakutat: There had been 12 men in the

settlement there, promyshlenniks under Larionov's command. Also there were some Kolosh of both sexes, who appeared to be loyal. They were used for work and as servants. It is not known whether by betrayal or treachery or in what other way Larionov, who had been so careful up until then, allowed the Kolosh to fall upon him suddenly. He and the other Russians died by torture. Only his wife, children and a few Aleuts survived.

Heartened by their success in destroying the Yakutat fort, the Kolosh prepared to go to Chugatsk and Kenai Bays and inflict the same fate on these forts. They set out in eight large baidaras. To obviate suspicion, they left six at the mouth of the Copper River and in the others travelled straight to Konstantinovsk fort, the chief settlement on Chugatsk Bay. Their toen Fedor, well known to the Russians as Baranov's devoted godson, appeared boldly before the fort's commandant, Uvarov, and declared that he had come to trade with the Chugach, as he often had before. Uvarov suspected nothing, but received him warmly, and allowed him to join in dancing with the Chugach.

On the baidaras left at Copper River there was a single captive Chugach who managed to escape and get news to Uvarov that the Kolosh had come not to trade but to destroy the Chugach and the Russians. As a result, Uvarov detained his breakfaith guest, toen Fedor, and said he knew all about his evil intentions. Meantime the Chugach, who had also already learnt of the plot, called all 70 Kolosh to join them in a feast and treacherously slew them all, except for two or three who fled. That night toen Fedor cut his throat and those who fled made their way to their remaining companions on the Copper River and told them what had befallen the others. This frightened the Kolosh, who feared that the Chugach were about to attack them also. They quickly got themselves together and in spite of stormy weather set off back across the sandbar which stretches far out

into the sea from the estuary of the Copper River. The
baidaras capsized on the bar in the heavy surf and many
of their people were drowned; a few managed to reach the
Ugaliakhmiut coast only to be killed there by the local
natives who were their traditional enemies.

For murdering the Russians in the settlement at
Yakutat the Kolosh received just punishment from the
Heavens. Of the 200 warriors who had set out hardly one
remained.

At the beginning of 1806, Rezanov undertook an
expedition to California, intending to acquaint himself
with the area and establish whether they could obtain
grain from that source and in what quantities. He
ordered Lieutenant Khvostov to prepare the Juno. To
Baranov he gave the task of loading goods for experiments in trade, to be at the disposal of Commissioner
Panaev. On February 26 the Juno left Sitka and arrived
at San Francisco where Rezanov met with Don José
Arrilaga, the Governor of California, and, with his permission, ordered some of his supplies to be bartered
with the San Francisco mission. The most important
goods obtained were: 671 fanegas of wheat,[43] 117 of
barley and 140 of peas and beans. In addition there
were flour, tallow, salt, and other items to the value
of 5,587 piasters, paid for in Russian and other goods.
He left the port of San Francisco on May 10 and returned to Sitka on June 8.[44]

Here Rezanov found that the tender, whose keel had
been laid at his instructions, had already been
launched, named Avos' and put under the command of
Davydov. It and the Juno both had crews made up of
young, brave, and healthy men. On June 24 Rezanov bade
farewell to Baranov, transferred to the Juno and on the
following day set sail.

Rezanov's plans to visit Japan are documented in
detail by Admiral A. Shishkov, in the preface to his
work on Khvostov and Davydov's travels. It not only
had no bearing on improving the state of affairs in the

colonies, but was a venture completely alien to Baranov.
The removal for two years or more of 60 of the best
workers on two vessels, deprived the colonies of vital
means of communication between the islands and left
many of Baranov's important designs incomplete. In the
meantime as all these workers were reckoned to be in
service, they had, by regulation, to receive their share
of the hunting profits, and the ship's officers and
assistants had to be paid. This caused much trouble and
discontent, especially among those who remained working
in the colonies, and frequently had to go without.

Possibly an interesting historical picture could
have emerged from the bold acts of Lieutenants Khvostov
and Davydov on certain Japanese islands, had they been
carefully and firmly controlled from the start and had
they not created such wretched consequences as the capture of brave Captain V. M. Golovnin. But for us, this
picture is obscured by a curtain of unpleasant memories,
and it will doubtless go into oblivion that way. Perhaps only the shy and incredible Japanese will leave to
posterity legendary tales of the Russians' deeds of
heroism.

While Rezanov was absent in California, the American
seafarer, John Winship, arrived in Sitka on May 6.
Baranov concluded an agreement with him on sea otter
hunting in the colonies, whereby Winship, taking aboard
his ship 50 baidarkas under the command of Slobodchikov,
set off to hunt along the coast of California. The
expedition was to last from 10 to 14 months. They ful-
filled the conditions, approached the shores of California, and began to hunt sea otter. They then crossed
to the nearby island of Seros (Lat. 28°2' N., Long. 115°
23' W.) There Winship and Slobodchikov disagreed and
quarreled. After this, Slobodchikov bought from the
Americans, for 150 sea otters, a small schooner which he
renamed the Nikolai. In her he set out with two hired
American assistants and three Sandwich Islanders for the
Sandwich Islands, and, from there, arrived in Sitka

in August. Winship followed him, arriving in September.
His total catch was 4,820 sea otters of all types, which
was then divided evenly.

The King of the Sandwich Islands, the famous Kamehameha [Tomea-mea], who had heard about Baranov's activities from American travellers, wanted to know him better
and, through Slobodchikov, he sent Baranov a gift of a
large helmet, and a cape from his own shoulders. The
cape was of shining red and yellow feathers, a mark of
his respect and good wishes. From then on, at various
intervals, they would send each other gifts through
American shipmasters.

In August, 1806, Baranov's old friend, the American
sea-captain O'Cain, arrived in Sitka on the Eclipse.
O'Cain brought him some false information. On the Sandwich Islands he had met the American Captain Soule, who
had just arrived from Canton. He claimed to have seen
Captain Lisianskii there, and to have learnt from him
that the Neva from Sitka had called at the Japanese port
of Nagasaki where she was permitted to exchange furs at
a good profit. Lisianskii then took the few furs left to
deliver there in December, and in February set out to
sail directly to Europe. To this O'Cain added that two
American ships had also put in to Nagasaki and, receiving permission, had traded very profitably. He also
reported that on the return voyage from Canton that Captain Soule had happened upon a vessel without steering
gear or masts, with a Japanese family on board. These
he had taken to the Sandwich Islands.

As though basing his argument on these pieces of
information, O'Cain suggested to Baranov that as an
experiment he be sent to trade in Nagasaki and to
deliver there the Japanese family. Baranov came to
terms with him on September 6, 1806. It was agreed that
O'Cain should make trading experiments, and that he
should establish close contacts with Nagasaki, Canton
and Batavia. The main points in the agreement were:
1) to collect from Sitka or Kad'iak, furs and goods for

trading in Japan at attractive prices, the profits made
on these to be divided evenly between the Company and
O'Cain: 2) to go to the Sandwich Islands for the
Japanese family and to deliver them to Nagasaki: to try
there to gain permission to trade, but if that were not
forthcoming then to go elsewhere: 3) in any port with
favorable trading conditions, to load up with as many
bartered goods as possible and to take them to Kamchatka:
to deliver part of the cargo there, and to bring the rest
back to Kad'iak. For the freightage O'Cain was to receive 70 piasters per ton for a heavy cargo, and 40 piasters per ton for a light one: 4) after unloading at
Kamchatka, to take aboard iron for Kad'iak, to be delivered at no cost: 5) the commissioner of the Company
cargo to be Bakadarov with some assistants: 6) any
expenses in Canton were to come out of the general
profits. In conclusion, it was stated that if the fur
prices in these places were lower than those set by the
Company, and yet the barter seemed favorable, so that the
return on the foreign goods would bring gains in Kamchatka and in the colonies, then O'Cain, who had taken no
part in the sale of the furs, would instead receive half
of the gains against the Kamchatka price, or most
decisively, double the freightage. Amongst the goods
O'Cain took on board were 1,800 sea otter pelts, 105,000
seals, 2,500 river beavers and other skins, whale bone,
and walrus tusks--in all valued at 310,000 rubles.
Baranov wrote to the Governor of Nagasaki, seeking
patronage from him and permission for trade, now and in
the future.

Setting out from Sitka, O'Cain called in at Kad'iak,
where he took on board a large cargo, and from there
travelled to the Sandwich Islands, and thence direct to
Canton. Baranov had instructed his commissioner to
appear in Canton before the Swedish Consul, Mr.
Ljungstedt, who received him kindly and warned him, in
Russian, against the deceitful manoeuvers of the Chinese
and even against O'Cain himself. This kindness on

Ljungstedt's part did not aid our inexperienced agent to
prevent O'Cain from getting very low prices, at which he
made it seem he was being forced to sell the furs. Sea
otters were reckoned at 13½ piasters, seals at 40 cents,
river beavers at 3 piasters, a pikul of walrus tusks at
25 and a pikul of whalebone at 10 piasters. At this
price scale the cargo was sold for 155,000 rubles, or
half the Company's estimate of its value. For it were
received 3,000 sacks of wheat, 280 chests of tea, 25,000
bolts of various sorts of kitaika cotton, much silk cloth
and cotton material, chinaware and a variety of other
Chinese goods.

On May 8, 1807, O'Cain left Canton and on July 6 he
sailed into Nagasaki Bay, under the Russian flag. Here
he was met by a multitude of small rowing craft, which
led the ship to anchorage. A Dutch official quickly
came out by tender, and finding that the Captain and the
crew were not Russian he advised them to change their
flag instantly because of Japanese indignation at a
recent Russian attack on their islands. O'Cain then
deemed it necessary to conceal Baranov's agents from the
Japanese. Six rowing boats were attached to the ship as
a guard. Their weapons and powder were removed, and
they were not allowed to communicate with shore.

To the questions of the Japanese, O'Cain asserted
that he had entered port because he needed fresh water
and provisions. The next day, by the order of the
authorities, sufficient fresh water, fish, pork, and
greenstuffs were brought to the ship, free of charge.
On the third day, O'Cain was escorted from the harbor by
Japanese vessels and on 8 July [August?] he arrived in
the port of Petropavlovsk.

In accordance with Baranov's instructions the
Kamchatka commissioner Miasnikov accepted the goods from
Bakadorov at a revaluation of 207,000 rubles. Finishing
the business in Kamchatka, O'Cain sailed to Kad'iak, but
near Sannakh Island he ran aground on a reef, and in the
night, the ship foundered. Almost all the cargo was

swallowed up by the sea. During 1808 O'Cain built a
small schooner from the fragments of his ship which had
washed up on shore. In it he set to sea on February 26
1809. But strong winds tore the sails from the schooner
and drove her onto the ice off Unalashka Island. The
ice damaged her seriously and knocked out her steering.
O'Cain, seeing no hope on the vessel, decided to abandon
her, and make his way over the ice to the shore, only
two miles distant. First he sent off Navigator Bubnov,
one Russian and nine Aleuts. When they had all safely
crossed the ice, O'Cain, two American sailors and a
Sandwich Island woman they had with them, set out to
follow in their tracks. But they were not so fortunate
as the first group, and all were drowned. The schooner,
heavily damaged by the ice and rocks, was washed up
nearby.

CHAPTER VII

After he sent O'Cain to Canton, Baranov found it
necessary to spend some time in Kad'iak. Leaving the
Novo-Arkhangel'sk fort stocked with foodstuffs and military supplies, he placed the garrison in charge of his
assistant Kuskov, and set sail on September 30, 1806.

Kuskov occupied himself with completing the fort
storehouses, a house for the Chief Manager, and other
buildings, while the diligent Lincoln repaired and built
boats. On March 4, 1807, he launched the beautiful brig
Sitka.[45]

Kuskov's lot was not very pleasant. The Kolosh,
learning that Baranov, whom they respected and feared,
had gone, began to plan an attack on the Russians, only
a small number of whom remained in the fort. They
gathered together from Chil'khit, Stakhin, Khutsnov,
Akoi, and other places. Under the pretext of herring
fishing, they occupied the islands surrounding the fort,
and in this fashion frightened and threatened the be-
sieged. According to Kuskov's observations and those of
his indefatigable colleagues, the number of hostile
savages reached (in 400 boats) more than two thousand.
The Russians, commending their souls to God, prepared to
withstand the siege. But this could prove a lengthy
business, and furthermore, the Aleuts were cut off from
fishing and fresh food supplies. The enemy knew our
men's intentions – in the fort were Kolosh maidens, who,
as they afterwards told the Russians, gave their fellow
countrymen information about both our numbers and forces,
and they intended to attack. This news was confirmed
when the Kolosh seized several Aleuts and, urging them
to treachery, promised them mercy and rewards when the
fort should be taken.

Kuskov had neither the forces nor the opportunity to
raise the siege or drive the enemy away. Knowing, however, that the Kolosh had great respect for the Chilkhat
toen, he decided either to use him as an intermediary or
to win his support. He sent specially to invite him to
come and visit with a worthy retinue, and this distinguished toen stepped importantly into the fort with a
following of 40 men. Kuskov honored and was kind to
these guests, and gave them gifts. In this way he persuaded them to leave the vicinity to avoid, as he told
them, the suspicion contained in rumors that their tribe
always had a friendly face, but evil intentions. The
toen was pleased with the reception and hospitality
afforded him by Kuskov. He renewed his former friendly
attitude, calling him his friend and soon, with all his
suite, he withdrew from the fort.

Probably this toen, with his forces, was the main
hope of the other Kolosh, because after he had gone they
all began to disperse and thus relieved the fort of the
unpleasant position it had been in.

Baranov's affairs in Kad'iak at that time included
various economic matters concerning development, regul-
ations and supply in the districts and in Sitka. However,
his presence in Kad'iak was mostly necessary because the
accountant in the office there had great difficulty in
compiling accounts of all the minute, but myriad conditions of hunting and profit sharing with the workers.
He had not been to Kad'iak for three years and in that
time the office had been run by Banner, a man with good
qualities, but very humble and pleasant to everyone.
This irrelevant pleasantness was the cause of various
orders and instructions not being carried out and, in
general, frustrating plans of the Chief Manager as well.

The vessel Sitka, stocked and sent off by Kuskov,
anchored at Kad'iak on May 2. There the English ship
Myrtle, under Captain Barber, had recently docked en
route from Bengal. Baranov purchased this ship complete
with cargo, for 42,000 piasters. Among the cargo were

some furs which Barber had bartered in the straits on
the Northwest Coast of America for 21,000 rubles: rum,
sugar, and other articles to the value of 38,000 rubles;
and artillery shells worth 4,000 rubles. In all, the
various parts of the cargo were worth 63,675 rubles.
Barber received a bill of exchange on the Company Main
Office and said he would deliver it to Okhotsk on a
Company transport. For this purpose Baranov chose the
newly completed brig Sitka, which, since she was late in
leaving Kad'iak, could not reach Okhotsk and called in
at Petropavlovsk. There, the agent Miasnikov loaded her
with the Canton wares, and sent her off to Nizhne-
Kamchatsk. As she was entering its estuary on October
3, 1807, the brig overturned on a sand bar and was
carried off to sea. The crew took to the boats, but all
of the cargo was lost. The ship bought from Barber was
renamed the Kad'iak. Under the command of Navigator
Bulygin she was sent from Kad'iak with foodstuffs for
Sitka, where she arrived on July 13. According to
Baranov's instructions, Kuskov sent the ship on to Yakutat to capture Kolosh there and to trade them for the
Aleuts and children who were still in captivity. On
September 13 Bulygin returned from Yakutat, reporting
that he had reached there from Sitka in five days and
raised a foreign flag. The toens, suspecting something,
did not visit the ships themselves, but sent a scouting
party of young girls in small boats. Bulygin succeeded
in seizing two of them and conducting talks through
them. From one toen, who swore that he had had no part
in the destruction of the fort, he managed to obtain
the manager Larionov's wife and three young sons and two
other wives and their children. To the demand for the
cannons and other articles the toen replied that they
had all been carried far off and could not quickly be
brought together again; about smaller articles he said
that they also had been divided amongst many of them
and he produced only a trunk with some papers, for which
he had no use. A year earlier Baranov had sent the

American Captain Campbell, who had seized the main
Chilkhat toen Asik, who controlled Yakutat, taken two of
his tribesmen as hostages, and ransomed out of captivity
an Aleut and his wife.[46]

On September 12, 1807, the ship Neva, under command
of Lieutenant Hagemeister, arrived in Sitka from St.
Petersburg. On the way she had visited San Salvador in
Brazil and Port Jackson in New Holland. She remained in
Sitka for some time and then went on to Kad'iak. This
ship brought Baranov the order of St. Anna, 2nd class,
in reward for his administration of the colonies; Kuskov
was awarded the rank of Commercial Counsellor.

A considerable quantity of goods and munitions were
unloaded under the supervision of Commissioner Zakharov.
The ship spent the winter in Kad'iak. At the beginning
of 1808, Lieutenants Kozliainov and Berg, Dr. Mordgorst,
and Commissioner Zakharov left the Company's service.
They were all sent back to Russia via Okhotsk.

The several experiments undertaken in sea otter
hunting with the foreigners in California, showed Baranov that considerable profits were to be made without
special preparations or expenses by the Company. He
therefore suggested that it become a regular practice.
The American captains were always on the lookout for ways
to make easy money, and, with this intent, were constantly appearing with proposals about joint sea otter
hunting. A renewed agreement (in May, 1808) with Captain
Ayres, the commander of the ship Mercury, already clearly
illustrates that it was not Baranov who sought it. It
consisted of the following points: 1) to give Ayres 25
baidarkas and for him to proceed to islands known only to
him for sea otter hunting: 2) the Company to provide two
prikashchiks to supervise the party, who were to eat at
the ship's table: 3) the Company to provide sustenance
for the Aleuts and if this were lacking they were to be
fed the ship's food: 4) the party of Aleuts were not to
be left without the protection of the ship's guns: 5) if
any of the Aleuts were taken captive or killed during the

hunting, then Ayres was obligated to pay their surviving
families 250 piasters each:[47] 6) the catch to be made
over to and held by the Company's appointee: 7) the
time allowed should be from 10 to 12 months: 8) on his
return the haul should be divided equally; Ayres for his
part should tender to the Company 3½ piasters per sea
otter to pay the Aleuts; for each koshlok [half-grown
sea otter] up to 1½ and for medvedki [sea otter pups]
up to a piaster each: 9) the furs obtained from the
savages by barter should be considered general property,
and the trade in California in Ayres' own goods should
be to his benefit. But if he were to buy grain and other
provisions, then he was to render them to the Company
at the prices agreed upon. The party was accompanied by
Shvetsov, as supervisor, and, according to his reports,
they left Kad'iak on June 27 and reached the Queen Charlotte Islands. Ayres there purchased some sea otters
from the Kolosh, paying for each one a keg of powder.
On June 15 they left the straits and sailed to the
Columbia River, where they encountered two United States
officials and some soldiers who had arrived overland.
They had already built a barracks. The officials were
distributing to the savages medals with Washington's
portrait. Here Shvetsov purchased 580 river beavers.
On August 31 they left the Columbia for the port of
Trinidad and thence to Bodego Bay and San Francisco on
December 1. From there they continued to sail south to
the port of San Diego, hunting sea otters, whenever the
weather permitted.

Having settled accounts, and put affairs in the
Kad'iak Section in order, Baranov decided to leave
Kad'iak altogether. But since it was in the center of
the colonies he left the main office there. He arrived
in Sitka on the Neva on August 30, 1808.

In his absence, at the beginning of 1808, Kuskov had
sent along the coast a party of Aleuts in 200 baidarkas
to hunt sea otters under the supervision of Slobodchikov,

and protected by the schooner Nikolai, which was
commanded by Benzeman.[48] The Kad'iak, under Bulygin,
was also sent there with goods to be bartered for sea
otters. Both ships returned together on July 20. The
Aleuts had caught 1,700 sea otters. But no barter agreement had been reached with the Kolosh because they wanted
mainly guns and powder, and asked too much for their own
goods.[49]

Lincoln had built a 300 ton ship with three masts.
It was launched on July 16, and given the name Otkrytie.
Soon afterwards the keel of a schooner was laid down.
This was called the Chirikov, in memory of the famous
Captain Chirikov, the first Russian to visit the North-
west Coast of America. Each craftsman who helped to
complete a vessel for the Company was paid a thousand
piasters.

Baranov knew about the natural produce of California
and the abundance of seals in that area from his agents
who had been sent there with American sea captains. Now
that there was a sufficient number of sailing ships, he
decided to send two of them off to California under the
general control of Kuskov. They were the schooner
Nikolai, commanded by Bulygin, on board which was the
prikashchik, Tarakanov, who was to supervise trade with
the savages, and the Kad'iak, commanded by Navigator
Petrov, on board which were Kuskov and a party of Aleuts.
The schooner left Sitka on September 20 for the Columbia
River in order to trade with the savages there. From
there she was to sail to Gray's Harbor where it had been
arranged that she should meet the Kad'iak. Near Gray's
Harbor they were shipwrecked, but all on board were
saved. To avoid hostile natives, they at first wandered
through the forests but were subsequently taken prisoner.
Their commander, Bulygin, died soon after, and the
prikashchik Tarakanov and a few of the promyshlenniks
returned to Sitka only in 1810, on an American ship.
Their sufferings were described in detail by the clever
Tarakanov and part of the account included by V. M.

Golovnin in the fourth part of his descriptions of famous shipwrecks.[50]

Kuskov left Sitka on October 15. Because of adverse winds he failed to reach Gray's Harbor and put in to Trinidad. Finding neither sea otters to hunt nor wares to be bartered for among the savages, he went to Bodego on December 28. There they caught 1,900 sea otters of various sorts. They left Bodego on August 18, 1809, but met almost constant northwest winds and could not make Sitka until October 4. After spending the spring and summer in California Kuskov brought Baranov fresh information about the riches and opportunities existing there --how suitable it was for cultivation, breeding cattle, and how rich in sea otters. Having respect for Kuskov's views and remembering the remarks made by Actual Chamberlain Rezanov that these regions did not as yet belong to any of the European powers, the enterprising Baranov proposed to the Main Office that they set up an establishment there, more for food production than for trading and hunting advantages.

In October, 1808, the Juno returned from Okhotsk; she had been delayed there by Lieutenant Khvostov's expedition to Japan. Then Baranov received the unpleasant news that the tender Avos', commanded by Lieutenant Sukin, and en route from Kad'iak to Sitka, had run aground and been wrecked in the Bay of Islands. The crew had been saved, but had remained there to watch over their belongings. Several of them volunteered to take the skiff to bring the news to Sitka. When they reached Sitka the sloop Konstantin, under the command of Navigator Il'in was quickly despatched to rescue them. This delivered them, and all the cargo that could be salvaged, to Novo-Arkhangel'sk.

In 1809, in Sitka, an unfortunate series of events took place which could have had the most dire consequences. Only the personal respect and devotion of some employees to the worthy Baranov restrained others who were troublemakers. Otherwise his life, so useful to the Company and not without fame for the Fatherland, might have come to a tragic and premature end.

Several stormy and deluded spirits, stupid ignoramuses who had no basic understanding of anything, had heard about the evil designs carried out on Kamchatka by the infamous Beniowski and, following his example, they decided to raise a rebellion in the colonies. The prikaz employee Naplavkov, exiled to settlement in Siberia, and subsequently a hunter, and another like him, the peasant Popov, were the main plotters. They managed to gather together ten men of like mind, telling them, amongst other things, that if the mutiny began successfully there would be many others who would join them. Their plan of action was as follows;.when it was Naplavkov's turn to stand guard in the fort, then he and two others should go to the Manager, who was always accessible to everyone, kill him and take charge of the guns in the fort and of the barracks.

The participants Leshchinskii, Berezovskii and Sidorov each informed Baranov about the plot, and of the fact that the plotters wished to bind all their fellows with their signatures, so that none of them should think of betrayal, or of turning evidence afterwards and escaping blame. Baranov thanked the informers for their loyalty and devotion, and desiring to discover more for himself and to catch the plotters red handed, he ordered Leshchinskii to ply them with vodka, and to tell him as soon as Naplavkov had written out their "agreement." Several days later, on July 26, the plotters met in the room shared by Leshchinskii and Berezovskii, which was near Baranov's quarters, and prepared to draw up the long-awaited list of signatures. Naplavkov, full of self importance, dictated it while Popov wrote it down, and when all had bound themselves by their signatures, Leschinskii sang a certain song as a pre-arranged signal to Baranov. Like a bolt from the blue, Baranov appeared with a group of armed men. The gallant Naplavkov, with a loaded pistol in one hand and his saber in the other,

suddenly lost his courage. Popov tore into small pieces
the list of names he had been holding. The mutineers
were seized and thrown in irons. The torn up pieces of
paper were carefully gathered and stuck together and
their contents then became clear. It disclosed that
they had chosen Popov as leader, to be obeyed by all,
but that they should do nothing until several important
colleagues arrived with a party from the straits.[51]

The inquiry conducted after these events revealed
that Naplavkov and Popov had chosen as their example the
actions in Kamchatka of Beniowski. The latter had
murdered Captain Nilov and plundered the treasury,
stolen a ship, and sailed to Canton. Naplavkov had been
in Kamchatka and heard a detailed account of all this.
In imitation of these evil deeds, they had proposed,
first of all, to murder Baranov and those living in the
house with him - namely Navigator Vasil'ev, the American
Clark, and Baranov's children. Then they were to turn
their attention to the barracks and the living quarters,
where they were to spare those who obeyed and joined
their band and were either to tie up or kill any who
remained loyal to Baranov. Then they were to take all
the richest furs and load them aboard the new ship
Otkrytie, which was armed, and sail out of Sitka. Their
guide was to be Navigator Shekhov with the apprentice
Voroshilov as his assistant. The former they hoped to
win over with threats or by force: if this were not
possible they were to seize the shipwright Lincoln,
assuming that he, as a foreigner, would more readily
agree to their proposals. Each plotter was commissioned
to take one young girl onto the ship with him, and in
addition to that 15 women. When they left Sitka they
intended to make for Easter Island or the uninhabited
islands lying to the south and settle there. If they
should lack provisions they were to go to the Sandwich
Islands where they could barter sea otters before the
news of their uprising became widespread. For the sea
otters they hoped to procure necessary goods and food.

confessing their intentions the mutineers could
not, then or subsequently, show or dream up any other
reasons for their dissatisfaction with Baranov apart
from the general shortage of food and the punishment of
several of them whom (as they thought) were innocent.

The chief instigators, Popov and Naplavkov, and four
of their colleagues, were kept in irons under guard and
sent for trial in Kamchatka with a report from Baranov
for the commandant of the oblast there.

The feeding of the crew of the ship <u>Neva</u>, which had
remained in the colonies, greatly taxed provisions.
Baranov therefore resolved, with the agreement of Captain Hagemeister, to send her to the Sandwich Islands,
there to stock up and load salt for Kamchatka and the
colonies.[52] In accordance with this proposal Captain
Hagemeister left Sitka on November 10, 1808 and, calling
first at Kad'iak, arrived at Oahu at the beginning of
January 1809. He stayed there three months, after which
he visited the islands of Maui and Kauai, loaded a considerable quantity of salt and arrived in the harbor of
Petropavlovsk on June 8.[53] Having there unloaded a
thousand puds of salt and a quantity of other supplies,
on July 20 he set sail, called in at Kad'iak and returned to Sitka on September 2.

At this time reliable reports were received from
Russia of the break with England. This now made it
impossible for the <u>Neva</u> to sail round the world to
Russia, and it was decided that she should winter at
Kad'iak and then Hagemeister would proceed to Kamchatka,
leave the ship in the port of Petropavlovsk under the
supervision of the commissioner there, and travel with
his crew by official transport ship to Okhotsk. On
September 21 the <u>Neva</u> sailed from Sitka. In April,
1810, it left Kad'iak and on May 29 arrived in Kamchatka. On it were the mutineers referred to already.

The plotting at Sitka was unpleasant for Baranov,
all the more so because the ringleaders were Russians
and, despite their confused aims and slim pretexts,

there was a chance that some suspicions, however slight, might fall on him. With advancing years he longed for the peace which should accompany age and regularly every year he besought the Company Directors to send him a successor. His willingness to give useful service had not slackened, but he naturally no longer had the ingenuity, speed and decisiveness which he had had in his prime, nor the strength to go everywhere and do everything himself. His earlier failures and misfortunes he had borne manfully and firmly in the hope and fervent intention of being able to recoup and improve on them, but now each ordeal sapped his failing strength still further and led, if not to desperation, then to somber sadness, for which there was nothing and no one to console him. He had not amassed a fortune, but had the honor and distinctions compatible to the rank into which he had been born. He had long wished for rest from his ceaseless cares and arduous labors, and longed only for peace in his homeland amongst those near and dear to him. Nevertheless, in spite of all his representation, he was persuaded by the Directors to take up his burden yet again in these familiar but harsh surroundings.

Baranov's administrative and directive affairs followed their normal course; he had most of his supplies from the Americans; the sea otter hunting continued, although with decreased expenses, but now not in such numbers from the colonies, but as a result of agreements made with foreigners. The parties of Aleuts sent out hunting along the coast from Sitka had nothing to equal their early successes. The Kolosh tried everywhere to prevent them from hunting and even the sea otters themselves, which had earlier inhabited the bays and inlets in such large herds, were now noticeably disappearing. The Kolosh hunted them with rifles, frightened them, and drove them away; the peace loving animals had sought shelter in some quieter place.

Communications by ship between the islands and Okhotsk were now in a happier state, with the exception

of the <u>Juno</u> which, sailing from Kad'iak under Benzeman,
ran into a savage storm on November 23, 1809. The
vessel's cargo, consisting mostly of foodstuffs which it
was difficult to pack firmly, shifted to one side, and
the ship took on a list. Then she lost her foremast,
anchor, three guns, and two men overboard. Not with-
standing all this, she arrived in Sitka on December 4;
Kuskov had travelled on her as a passenger.

CHAPTER VIII

On June 30, 1810, the naval sloop _Diana_ arrived in
Sitka from Kamchatka under the command of Captain-
Lieutenant V. M. Golovnin, on a mission entrusted to
this worthy officer by the High Government. During his
stay in port, about August 3, the American Captain Brown
brought in the prikashchik Tarakanov, whom he had rescued from captivity and whose adventures have been
described above.

In July, the American vessel _Enterprise_, under
Ebbets, arrived from New York with a cargo of merchan-
dise. The Consul General (afterwards the accredited
Ambassador to the United States and Actual State
Counsellor) Andrei Iakovlevich Dashkov, now discovered
that Baranov was short of supplies in the colonies, that
he bought them from various American seafarers and had
no permanent contact with the best trading houses. He
recommended him in a letter to Mr. Astor, a prominent
businessman in New York, who agreed to have a permanent
contact with our colonies, and being the director of a
fur company, himself intended to establish a settlement on the Columbia River.

Mr. Astor also wrote to Baranov from New York that:

> during a residence of around 25 years in this
> city he had traded solely in furs and had
> until now had more dealings with the Canadian
> Company, shipping their wares to Europe and
> Canton; that now, having reached agreement
> with Ebbets, he had decided to send the first
> ship to trade on the Northwest Coast of
> America. While this was being prepared he had
> met Mr. Dashkov, had changed his plans and had
> had the boat loaded with wares necessary to
> and useful in our colonies. In sending this
> boat off direct he gave complete authority to
> Captain Ebbets to negotiate, reach conditions,

enforce contracts if necessary, with two or
three ships to supply our colonies each year,
and so forth.[54]

When Baranov received this proposal he bought needed
goods from Ebbets for 27,000 piasters, paying him in
furs; but he refrained from concluding a contract for
the future, claiming that the war with England could
not be a lengthy one, and after that, of course, the
Main Office would send everything he needed from St.
Petersburg. In his answer to Astor he mentioned "that
at his own request he hoped soon to be relieved of his
duties and could not therefore conclude any permanent
obligations, but he had compiled a list of requirements,
at commonly accepted prices, which could be carried in
one or two ships as cargo forwarded to him."

Taking advantage, however, of the chance of having
permanent contacts with one of the foremost businessmen
in the United States, Baranov suggested to Ebbets that
he sail to Canton and there barter Company furs for
various goods needed in the colonies. Ebbets readily
agreed to this proposition and on June 20, 1810, an
agreement was concluded, the main points of which were
as follows: 1) to despatch Company fur goods to the
value of 65,000 piasters: 2) the sale of these furs
and the purchase in Canton of Chinese goods needed by
the colonies was to be entrusted to the honor of Ebbets
because of his special devotion towards the worthy Mr.
Astor: 3) as commission for the sale and purchase of
goods in Canton, Ebbets was offered 5% of the actual
turnover: 4) for delivering the furs to Canton and returning with the Chinese goods he would receive from the
Company 18,000 piasters. Of this sum he would receive a
third in Canton from the sale of the furs, and the
remainder when he returned to Sitka: 5) all expenses in
Canton, whatever they might be, Ebbets would bear himself; and finally he was obliged to render to Baranov
a fair set of accounts. Ebbets' cargo included 3,000
sea otters, 3,000 beaver tails, 100 puds of whale bone,

66,000 seals, several fox furs, land otters, river
beavers, and walrus tusks--in all at 145,000 rubles.

In July, Ebbets left Sitka and sailed to Canton
where he conducted his trade, returning in May 1811.
The furs had been sold fairly profitably, the sea otters
at 21½ piasters each, the beaver tails for two piasters,
the [land] otters for four, the seals for one, and river
beavers for about 6½ piasters each. In return had been
received 100 cases of lump sugar, 1,000 pikuls of wheat,
8,000 bolts of cotton, 520 chests of tea, 100 cases of
tea and 14 of table china, 1,200 bolts of various silk
materials, and a quantity of smaller articles--in all to
the value of 64,000 piasters.

When he had received accurate accounts Baranov was
certain of Ebbets' sense of honor and justice, and was
very pleased with the trading deal which had brought
much profit to the Company and the inhabitants of the
colonies, when measured against earlier prices. When
these goods had been received, a general tariff was
established at which the goods were to be sold in the
colonies. I attach here a list of the prices, which
until that time had not been fixed for some of the more
important articles and supplies:[55]

ARTICLE	WEIGHT	RUBLES	KOPEKS
Sugar lumps	pud	16	00
Rice	pud	5	50
Cotton, flesh colored	bolt	3	00
" fine weave	"	4	00
" black wide	"		
" wide measure	"	8	80
Demi cotton	bolt	5	00
Bengal cotton, fine	bolt	22	00
Velvet	bolt	89	60
Thread	pound	3	00
Tea utensils	chest	12	00
Table china	chest	80	00
Tea, green, first grade	pound	2	25

ARTICLE	WEIGHT	RUBLES	KOPEKS
Tea, green, normal	pound	1	70
" " black leaf	pound	2	00
" " suchong	pound	1	30
Taffeta	bolt	29	00
Fanza [Foulard]	bolt	22	00
Kanfa [Satin]	bolt	65	00
Kancha silk	bolt	42	00

Apart from the goods bartered in Canton, Baranov brought another 35,000 piasters worth of English goods from Ebbets, also paid for in furs, with which Ebbets again set out for Canton.

Over and above the articles received from Ebbets and bartered in Canton, Baranov also bought a significant quantity from other sea captains, and when he had built up surplus stocks, decided to send some to Kamchatka. For this purpose he ordered the Juno to be made ready, and placed under the command of Navigator Martynov. He sent her to sea in July. We shall follow her to Kamchatka.

The richly laden ship did not reach her destination: she was wrecked not far from the port of Petropavlovsk near the mouth of the Viliui River November 3, 1811. Only three of the crew were saved. Afterwards they discovered, washed up by the sea, a report by the ill-fated captain, which he had prepared for the Company's commissioner. Here is an extract from it:

With the vessel entrusted to me I have arrived from the port of Novo-Arkhangel'sk in the most wretched condition. I have been sailing for three months from the Northwest Coast of America and struggling against almost unending storms. Now already in sight of the shore here for 19 days, I have only 3 sailors and they exhausted, and 5 young apprentices whom I brought with me for training; of them, the two oldest perform sailors' duties in addition to their own. The other three take the wheel, bail out water (which comes aboard during strong winds at the rate of 5 inches every hour) throw out the

lead sounder and keep the ship's journal.
Sailing a three masted ship with these 8
people is a difficult undertaking, the
rest of my crew....

and this is where the exhausted seafarer ends his report.
Those who were saved completed the picture. During the
last storm the steering gear and chains had been torn
away and the bulwarks stove in. After this they drifted
for a little while along the coast hoping to find some
kind of bay on the coast of Kamchatka. In this they at
last succeeded and anchored in 35 sazhens, but the wind
strengthened and the ship began to drag its anchor; they
threw out the second anchor but the cable broke and the
ship was thrown on a reef parallel to the shore. There
the giant waves smashed on her fiercely but briefly;
probably it was the tide and increasing swell which
threw her across the reef and onto another nearer the
shore.

The extraordinarily strong surf beat upon the ship
with terrible force, huge waves came aboard, breaking
over her, ruining everything above decks. The timbers
cracked at every blow. The seafarers, numb with fear
and cold, hung on wherever they could. One wave washed
away six men who had been hanging on the rigging,
amongst them the Captain. After many similar blows,
each washing away more men, the boat was thrown over
the reef, dashed against the rocky shore at the mouth
of the Viliui River and knocked onto its side. Of the
22 man crew at that moment, only four remained, clinging
to the shrouds. In this dreadful situation the ship
remained for six hours constantly washed over by the
waves and driven closer to shore. Then one of the
sailors, who had some strength left, climbed out onto
the main mast, and, by holding onto pieces of the ship
which were jammed against the rocks, clambered out onto
the cliff face. Wet through and numbed, he fell onto
the rocks exhausted. His imperilled comrades, seeing
him safe, took heart, summoned their last remaining

strength, and followed his brave example; two successfully clambered up onto the cliffs but the third was
covered from view by a wave, and...was gone.

The survivors thanked God for their deliverance,
but when they had rested they saw with grief that their
sufferings were only going to continue. Any moment they
might have become victims of hunger or cold, or food for
wandering bears, hungry at that time of year, but they
stumbled upon some fisherfolk who lived on the river's
edge not far away. These received the survivors with
consideration and kindness for their lot, and subsequently delivered them to the harbor at Petropavlovsk.

When he received news of this from Petropavlovsk the
Company Commissioner [Khlebnikov] and Lieutenant Podushkin immediately set out for the scene of the shipwreck.
There by the Viliui River, they found for a distance of
three versts along the shore the limbless and disfigured
corpses of their comrades, covered in sand and seaweed;
some were even caught in the branches of the trees, but
most terrible of all was the spectacle of those lifted
up by the waves and thrown against the cliffs and
hanging there by an arm or leg, their whole body in the
air. Nine corpses were discovered and buried. Lumps
and tatters of the cargo littered the seashore and the
river's edge. Let us draw a veil over this awful
picture and turn our attention again to the main scene
of action.

In October, 1811, the brig _Maria_ arrived in Sitka,
under command of Kuritsyn, who had been sent from
Okhotsk with men and supplies in 1810 and had wintered
in Kamchatka. Also on this vessel had been Collegiate
Assessor Koch, appointed assistant to Baranov with a
view to his taking over the Chief Managership once he
had got into the swing of things, and to thus release
Baranov to return to Russia. Koch was already an old
man and before reaching his proposed destination, he
died at Petropavlovsk Harbor on January 25, 1811.

For Baranov this news was doubly grievous, for Koch

had been an old friend and had constantly been on close terms with him.[56]

Baranov, meanwhile, at his own request, had received permission from the Main Office, approved by the Higher Administration, to found a settlement in New Albion, at whatever place he should deem most suitable. The northern part of Bodego Bay, although not altogether safe for ships, was, at least, promising. Baranov proposed that it be occupied and renamed Count Rumiantsev Bay as a sign of respect for the Company's patron and State Councillor. For the settlement however, adhering to the choice and suggestion of Kuskov, who had been there, he agreed on a spot 18 miles north of the original bay, because it was richly surrounded by all kinds of forests suitable for building, meadows for pasturing cattle, and soil for cultivation, as well as a supply of fresh water in the stream flowing there. These advantages were lacking in Count Rumiantsev Bay.

For constructing the new settlement, 25 Russian craftsmen and the necessary materials were allocated Kuskov, and 40 baidarkas were given with Aleuts for sea otter hunting and to assist in the work at the initial opening of the settlement. In November, 1811, these men set out from Sitka on the schooner Chirikov under the command of Benzeman.

At the beginning of 1812, Kuskov prepared construction timber and in June founded Ross settlement (Lat. 38° N. and Long. 123° 15' W. from Greenwich) on the slopes of a hill rising more than 120 feet above sea level. The fort was surrounded by a standing stockade 49 sazhens long and 42 wide. Inside were built a house for the manager, barracks, storehouses, and other structures.

The American Spaniards were amazed to see a people of whom they had only heard so far, now become close neighbors. While the Californian authorities were treating with Kuskov about the settlement and reporting

to the Mexican Viceroy, Kuskov had met and gained the
sympathy of the missionaries and those in control of
neighboring lands. He purchased from them cattle, seeds
and poultry and with this stock their economy was
established.

Baranov together with American skippers, continued
to hunt sea otters letting the Americans have as many
baidarkas as they needed, under supervision of his
assistants. The following are the accounts for the
year 1812:

Year of agreement	Captains	Vessels	No. of baidarkas	No. of sea otters rec'd as the Company's share
1809	John Winship	O'Cain	50	2,728
1810	Nathan Winship	Albatross	68	560
	William Davis	Isabella	48	2,488
1811	Thomas Meek	Amethyst	52	721
	Wm. Blanchard	Katherine	50	758
1812	Whittemore	Charon		896
			Total	6,149

Thus this trading brought the Company more than
7,000 sea otters in three years. The rules governing it
had already been laid down. It is clear on the one
hand that the profits were shared with foreigners, but
on the other the hunting took place predominantly outside the colonies, which were, by now, denuded of sea
otters. The Americans with an eye to profits valued
Baranov's goodwill. Many of them both then and later
referred to him with the greatest gratitude and praise.

In mid-January 1813, a sloop appeared in Sitka with
several of our sailors worn out by hunger and cold.
They told Baranov that the ship Neva which had left
Okhotsk in the previous year under Lieutenant Podushkin (on which was also the man appointed to replace
Baranov as Chief Manager of the colonies, T. S. Bornovolokov, Collegiate Councillor), had been forced by

adverse winds to abandon attempts to reach Sitka by
autumn, and had put in at Voskresensk Harbor. From
there she had sailed under Navigator Kalinin and on the
night of January 9 had been wrecked off Cape Edgecumbe.[57]
The drowned included Bornovolokov, the ship commander
Navigator Kalinin, the wife and son of Navigator Nerodov,
the cadet Terpigorev, a prikashchik and 21 promyshlen-
niks--of these, three had been seriously injured on the
rocks and soon died. On the journey from Okhotsk many
fell ill with scurvy because of damp weather, and thus
at various times 15 people died.

Baranov, now having spent 23 years in the colonies,
in the 67th year of his active life, awaited daily for
a replacement to release him, to at last lift from him
the burden of responsibility he had borne for so long.
With the growth of the colonies the task had already
become too much for a feeble old man. The news of the
latest mishap and Bornovolokov's fate inevitably made
him suffer spiritually, and rage against a cruel destiny
which had twice deprived him of a long and eagerly
awaited successor--who had been so near. He had constantly complained that the Company had disregarded his
urgent requests to be replaced, but the dispatch of two
Managers, one after the other, had nullified this. They
had met his requests, but Providence had disposed otherwise. Humble always before the will of the Almighty,
Baranov no longer struggled and continued to fulfill his
duties with the same zeal as before.

The survivors also brought the sad news of the cap-
sizing of the brig Aleksandr which had been sent to
Okhotsk. She had sailed from Sitka in June 1812 under
Navigator Petrov, carrying a rich cargo, including 8,000
sea otters. She was wrecked on the southwest side of
the fifth Kurile Island (Onekotan). All the crew and
part of the cargo were saved. Baranov decided to send
Lieutenant Podushkin to Kamchatka to carry goods there
along with the cargo, furs, and men saved from the
Aleksandr. In May, Podushkin left Sitka on the Otkrytie,

visited Unalashka, and called at Petropavlovsk Harbor.
She wintered there, received a prikashchik from Commissioner Iudin who went with her to the Kurile Islands
and there loaded men and cargo. On June 1 they
approached Onekotan, in the fourth Kurile strait, and
sent off two baidaras with 22 men to the island. Soon
a thick fog settled which held for four days and nights.
All this time Podushkin lay off the island and signaled
by gunfire, but as he received no answer, he decided to
make for Okhotsk.

The baidaras sent from the vessel reached the fifth
island and there found the salvaged cargo of 2,300 sea
otter pelts and 2,500 fox furs under guard by appointed
survivors—the remainder had been transferred earlier to
Kamchatka. In the fog they had not heard the signal
shots. When it cleared, the ship was gone and they had
to remain on the deserted island and wait their chance
to cross to the second island. Because they had
expected to be off the ship only for a short while, they
had not taken clothes nor food, and therefore had to eat
roots, grasses and shellfish for more than a month. Then
need decided them: without waiting for the ship any
longer, they loaded all the furs they could into their
boats and set off in fine weather through the fourth
strait to the second island and then further. They were
lucky enough that on September 1 they safely reached the
mouth of the Bol'shaia River.

Meantime war had broken out between England and the
United States. The American skippers trading in the
straits, in California, Peru and the Southern Ocean, in
fear of British cruisers, were constantly calling in at
Sitka and offering their wares and ships to Baranov at
bargain prices. Many wares were bought from them for
sealskins.

Astor, wishing to support his trading relations with
Baranov, sent the ship Tonquin from New York with a rich
cargo, instructing her to call at the Columbia River,
where he had already established a settlement,[58] then to

go to Sitka, having first tried trading with the
savages on the Northwest Coast of America. These savages, supplied with firearms by the "humanitarian"
Europeans, and especially by Astor's compatriots,
seized on the Captain's carelessness: They attacked
the ship, killing everyone, plundering the cargo, and
setting the ship on fire. Our Ambassador Plenipotentiary in the United States told Baranov of these events.
He also reported that Mr. Astor had sent another ship
for our colonies and that the new settlements in the
Ohio region, on the Mississippi River, were flourishing,
that settlements were spreading to the upper reaches of
the Missouri River, and that there would soon be un-
hindered communications between the States and the
Columbia River.[59]

The Lark, under Captain Norton, sent from New York
by Astor, was wrecked in the Sandwich Islands in 1813,
and her rich cargo, intended for Sitka, was largely
lost.

Because the sealskin trade was unprofitable and
they were then in slight surplus in Russia, Baranov
preferred to sell them to the Americans, buying in return goods, and even ships themselves. During 1813, in
addition to various cargoes, he bought from Captain
Bennet goods worth 31,000 piasters, and for 20,000
seals the two ships, Atahualpa and Lady, fully armed.
The first, a three master, was renamed the Bering, in
honor of the first Russian navigator in the Eastern
Seas; and the other, a brig built of East Indian teak
renamed the Il'mena.

Baranov now had more vessels than men to command
them, so he took into Company service from American
ships the Englishman Young and the American Vozdvit [?]
giving the latter command of the Il'mena. He was
assigned to take goods and supplies to Fort Ross, and
then go on to hunt sea otters along the California
coast. For this purpose a party of Aleuts was sent on
the brig under Tarakanov's supervision, and the

American Doctor Elliot, who had also entered Company service and offered Baranov his aid along the coast of California trading with the missionaries and inhabitants, whom he had long known.

This expedition sailed in December 1813. Elliott delivered the supplies to Ross, and then traded profitably at San Francisco. There he loaded bread grains and other provisions and delivered considerable quantities to Kuskov, the administrator at Ross. Then he continued sailing along the California coast, selling goods for cash, and also delivered to Kuskov more than 10,000 piasters to send to Sitka; all this time the Aleuts were hunting sea otters.

The California government had long been watching the movements of Elliot and the hunting party. One day, standing off Point Conception, he went ashore to trade, and the Aleuts had to hunt when they were attacked by mounted soldiers. Elliot, some Russian promyshlenniks and about 30 Aleuts were taken prisoner. Some of the Aleuts who escaped brought the news to the ship, which then went to Ross. There, loading more wheat, she set to sea again. On the voyage she sprang a leak and they were forced to put in at the Sandwich Islands.[60]

CHAPTER IX

When purchasing wares and vessels from Bennet,
Baranov had no seals on hand to pay him with, so by
agreement Bennet and some assistants left Sitka in April
1814, for Paul Island. Collecting some seals there, he
went to Okhotsk and got more than half a million rubles
for the furs sent over from Sitka. There he received
dispatches and with six hunters he sailed to the Sandwich Islands where he had been commissioned to buy taro
root, tutui nuts for extracting oil, salt and other
supplies. When he had bought necessities on Oahu [Voaga]
he anchored at Kauai Island, went ashore and arranged to
spend the night there. Overnight a strong wind sprang
up, the ship was blown ashore and wrecked. During this
disaster Kaumualii, ruler of Kauai Island, gathered on
shore with his suite, and Kaumualii told Bennet that he
had given orders to salvage the cargo and keep it in
safe storage. When this had been done, however, the
King declared that according to their custom everything
washed up on shore belonged to him. Bennet could not
dissuade the King from this injustice; and was forced to
leave on an American ship. The six Russians who had
been brought from Okhotsk were fed at the King's pleasure, but when their clothes wore out they walked around
like the islanders, until Captain Smith arrived, en
route for Sitka, and took them there with him.

All of Baranov's ventures and attempts to form
trading relations with the peoples of the Pacific
Eastern Ocean failed; but he still hoped to develop
permanent trading in some port or other. Experience had
already shown that in Canton and Nagasaki this was hope-
less; but the need for Chinese goods forced him to try
Manila. To this end he formed with the respected

American businessman Davis, to collect goods and an
agent of his from Sitka, and to go to Manila, to arrange
for Davis to accept local produce and Chinese goods
there. Davis left Sitka on the ship Isabella on June 9,
1814, but this expedition never lived up to expectations.
In Manila then there were no trading houses, nor supplies of products for cargo, so they had to return
empty handed.

With the end of war in Europe the ship Suvorov was
sent from St. Petersburg and reached Sitka on November
17 1814, under command of Lieutenant M. D. Lazarev with
a cargo of various wares. It was intended that she
should [merely] winter there, but despite the quantities
of goods awaiting transport back to Russia, Baranov proposed fetching sealskins from the Pribylov Islands. For
this reason the Suvorov left Sitka on May 7, collected
the cargo, and returned to Sitka on June 14. Apart from
the sealskins, various furs on hand were loaded for
shipping to Russia, and the Suvorov left the colonies on
July 24.[61] En route, she called at San Francisco in
California and the Peruvian port of Callao, where
quantities of Peruvian produce were loaded, partly
through barter and partly on guarantee - they included
Peruvian bark (quinine), ratania, sarsaparilla, and other
goods which were conveyed to Russia.

Apart from the furs despatched on the Suvorov,
Baranov also had a considerable quantity in store for
the Kiakhta trade. These were sent on July 9 1815 on
the brig Maria, under command of Navigator Petrov. She
reached Okhotsk safely and stopped there in the roads
before entering harbor. Suddenly a gale blew up from
the sea, making the brig drag her anchors, and prevent-
ing her from entering the river mouth. The ship's commander, fearing lest they run onto the rocks, decided to
sail her out into a better position and straight onto
the sloping, sandy beach. The strong surf beating upon
the ship drove her onto shore. The cargo and crew were
saved, but the brig was left useless. Out of a cargo

valued at 800,000 rubles, very little had been lost.

From the Suvorov a Doctor Sheffer, who had good
knowledge of English and French remained behind in the
colonies. To Baranov he seemed the right man to make an
expedition to the Sandwich Islands to investigate the
wreck of the Bering. Captain Bennet who had lost the
Bering, was then in Sitka, and urged Baranov to demand
compensation by force of arms. But Baranov would not
countenance hostilities against Kamehameha, the King of
the Sandwich Islands whose vassal was Kaumualii, ruler
of Kauai. He proposed that Doctor Sheffer should arrive
posing as a researcher in natural history, and travel on
a foreign vessel, to avoid raising even the slightest
suspicion. Sheffer's actual commission was to seek from
Kamehameha an order compelling Kaumualii to compensate
the Company for its loss and, if this were successful to
proceed with concluding permanent trading relations with
the islands. Baranov well knew that, because of the
proximity of the Sandwich Islands, he should long ago
have established there a factory to receive and process
local produce needed in the colonies, which would be
cheaper than that secured from foreign ships. The
islands could provide rum, tobacco, the nutritious taro
root – used instead of bread – pork, salt, and tutui
plants from which oil might be obtained; tackle from
coconuts, and thread from wooden fibers which were
especially useful for seine nets and sea otter nets;
fresh fruit and so forth.

Baranov at this stage had no assistants to whom he
could delegate all this work. Banner was administering
Kad'iak and Kuskov was at Ross. Moreover, Doctor
Sheffer's readiness in volunteering his services could
leave no doubt of his eagerness and abilities. Possibly
Baranov had not properly evaluated all sides of the
doctor's character. He realised, of course, that zeal
and ardor must be balanced by good sense, steadfastness
and knowledge of the matter in hand, but would be

hampered by idle dreams and promises, maladroitness and
flattery.

Sheffer set off on the foreign ship _Isabella_ on
October 5 1815. Two vessels, the _Otkrytie_ and the
Kad'iak, were to follow him, carrying goods to be exchanged for Sandwich Island produce. The _Otkrytie_,
under Lieutenant Podushkin, left Sitka on March 3, and
the _Kad'iak_, under Young, on March 24 1816.

When he arrived at Hawaii, Sheffer had met with King
Kamehameha and since he had letters of introduction from
Baranov, he was confident of the King's welcome and presented the claim against Kaumualii. The King promised
to order that the Company should be compensated for the
loss. In addition, Kamehameha, in token of respect for
Baranov's wishes and since he had long wanted to know
him better, let Sheffer choose for Baranov several
places in his territories for buildings. He ordered
a lake stocked with fish and several plantations to be
set aside on Lanai Island, and on Oahu, at the port of
Honolulu, a portion of land and a similar lake. Here
Sheffer built a small house, and planted tobacco, maize,
water melons, melons, marrows, and other useful plants.

On April 21 the _Otkrytie_ arrived, and on the 30th,
the brig _Il'mena_ from California, under command of
Vozdvit [?]. This brig from Bodego had been sailing to
Sitka with a cargo of salt, wheat and processed sea
otter pelts, and had sprung a leak. As they had not
dared to enter any hostile Californian port, they made,
as has already been said, for the Sandwich Islands,
without knowing that Doctor Sheffer was there. This
vessel was unloaded at Honolulu. The damage and loss to
the cargo, from the leak, included 500 puds of salt and
around 500 puds of wheat.

Leaving an agent and some Aleuts behind to guard the
newly acquired land on Oahu, Sheffer sailed to the
island of Hawaii on May 4 on the _Otkrytie_. Once there,
he obtained from King Kamehameha the order to Kaumualii
and, thus armed, went to Kauai on May 17. King

Kaumualii received Sheffer cordially, promising to return to the Company all the cargo salvaged from the
Bering. He wished to conclude an agreement about the
sandalwood trade and he also gave land in various places
on the island for plantations and building factories.

Sheffer, giddy with these unexpected successes and
Kaumualii's favorable reception, had visions of profit-
ing even further. He suggested that the King seek the
protection of the mighty power of Russia, agreeing to
act in its interests, and so forth. The King, little
comprehending the meaning of all this, accepted the proposal and agreed without hesitation.

Again leaving a prikashchik and some Aleuts on this
plantation as guards, Sheffer several days later returned to Hawaii to complete his almost lunatic schemes.

On May 31 they sailed in the Otkrytie; but the next
day they met a fierce storm, in which they lost the
mainsail and mizzen masts. Showing some false armaments
Podushkin limped to Niihau Island and anchored offshore.
He put Sheffer ashore and, when he had received enough
food for the journey to Sitka, he decided to go straight
there. He left the islands on the 13th and after a
happy voyage reached Novo-Arkhangel'sk on July 17.

Sheffer crossed by baidarka from Niihau to Kauai.
He lived with the King and with the Sandwich Islanders
he had been given as workers, built a factory and worked
the plantation. The headlong speed with which, ignoring
everything, he began to trade and give instructions on
the islands, antagonized the North American traders who
had dealings with the Sandwich Islands. They began to
convince Kamehameha that Kaumuali had sold out to
Russians and was concealing the fact from him, and that
Doctor Sheffer had taken over all Kauai and was building
forts there.[62] It is not surprising that these rumors
which were partially true, were embellished and exagger-
ated. Sheffer's actual instructions were to bind
Kaumualii to offer the Company all the sandalwood from
his islands. On Kauai, near where the Bering was

wrecked, he had two grass huts built and from material aboard the Otkrytie and that salvaged from the Bering a wooden house, as a factory. On the promontory an area 300 sazhens long and 15 wide was marked off with a mud and rock stockade as a fort. A small gun emplacement was built. The house had a garden 60 sazhens long and 15 wide, which held an orange tree. Mainly as an experiment, cotton, sugar cane, pineapples, melons, watermelons, and other fruits were sown.

To please the King the doctor bartered or bought for him a schooner, in which he sailed to Oahu to discuss payment for her. There, open hostility broke out between Sheffer and the Englishman Young, King Kamehameha's favorite and adviser. As a result the impetuous doctor was told that, for the peace of the island of Oahu, he should leave and give all his possessions to Kamehameha. The vessel Kad'iak, which had arrived at Oahu from Sitka, sprang a leak in the harbor and sank. Her captain, Young, was transferred to the Il'mena, on which he sailed to Kauai.

Subsequently, on April 17 1817, Kaumualii seized Sheffer, wrecking all his schemes for the Sandwich Islands, and handed him over to an American ship, on which he was taken to Canton.

The brig Il'mena returned to Sitka on June 17 1817, bringing Baranov news of Sheffer's headstrong behavior and pipe dreams. He had been unable to complete his schemes, and instead of developing trade and recouping losses as originally intended, the Company had suffered yet another misfortune and sustained very heavy losses, which on a monetary basis alone came to more than 200,000 rubles.

If this agent of Baranov's had been more circumspect and cautious and had negotiated more moderately and skillfully, he would first have received those small plantations on Oahu and Kauai and later if things went well, would not only have established but maybe even enlarged them. In the meantime, gaining the people's

love by his kind behavior and winning the trust of the
foreigners, he would probably have been showered with
praise and received his due rewards. Baranov's far
sighted and sound intentions would have brought him
special honor. But the opposite transpired: Sheffer's
ill timed attempts to take trade and local produce into
his own hands, to squeeze out foreigners, and finally,
to undermine the power of the King himself, roused
universal anger and indignation. Baranov, however,
carried the blame for him, although he had never had the
slightest intention of seizing the islands or seeking
exclusive trade. He had made a mistaken and rash choice,
and he paid dearly for it. The sneers and insults from
his fellow countrymen, poisonous reproaches from the
foreigners and the loss of Company money affected the
old man's pride. He was long tortured by remorse over
his choice of Sheffer.[63]

Affairs in the colonies ran their normal course.
From the new settlement in Albion, Kuskov travelled on
the Chirikov to the neighboring Spanish port of San
Francisco, and bartered there with the missionaries for
grain, sending a total of 6,000 puds to Sitka in 1815
and 1816.

In February, 1818, the Chirikov, under Benzeman, was
sent to Monterey with Lieutenant Podushkin aboard. He
was delegated to ask the Governor of California to
return the Aleuts who had been taken prisoner while
hunting, and to buy grain. De Sola, respecting his
representations, ordered two Russians and twelve Aleuts
to be set free and let food stuffs be exchanged in
requisite quantities which the Chirikov carried to Sitka
on June 12. Several Aleuts who had become Catholics and
married Indian girls, elected to remain at the missions
where they had initially been lodged.

From the very beginning of Ross settlement, the returns from sea otter hunting were meager. From 1812 to
1817 only about one thousand sea otters were caught in
all. In the following years no sea otters appeared near

the settlements and the hunters could not enter Spanish
ports for fear of incidents. Thus, in order to promote
gainful employment in Ross, Kuskov, with Baranov's
permission, laid down a brig and also introduced crop
and livestock farming.

On Baranov's representations to the Main Office of
the Company, a priest arrived in Sitka in 1816 with
church vessels. Churches were then established, and
the Holy Faith shone out across the wasteland of Northwest America only recently discovered by the Russians,
and made theirs by the tireless and unceasing efforts
and heroic deeds of Baranov.

On July 23, 1817, the ship _Suvorov_ arrived in Sitka
under Lieutenant Ponafidin, and on November 20, the
Kutuzov, under Captain-Lieutenant Hagemeister, who had
visited these parts before. En route these vessels had
called at Lima. The _Suvorov_ had come directly from
there, while the _Kutuzov_ had called at several coastal
ports in Peru, crossed to Bodego Bay, then called at
San Francisco, where a large stock of food supplies had
been purchased for the colonies. The cargoes of these
ships consisted of a rich stock of stores and ships'
materials, worth approximately half a million rubles.

Baranov was pleased with the supplies and other
necessities from California. But he was angered and
openly protested that the Company had ignored his persistent requests, and refused to replace him, forcing
him to continue under his heavy burden. His frequent
complaints eventually persuaded Captain Hagemeister to
himself assume the duties of Chief Manager of the
colonies, for which he had been provisionally granted
powers by the Main Office. But for personal reasons he
long hesitated, reluctant to accept these new and
arduous duties, strewn with so many cares, worries and
discords. One circumstance seemingly decided him to
act: the respected and tireless S. I. Ianovskii, first
lieutenant on the _Suvorov_, was courting Baranov's
daughter and had agreed to remain in Sitka for two years.

Most of the newly arrived goods had been delivered
to Baranov and the Suvorov was loaded with furs and
ready to depart when Captain Hagemeister, having decided
to take over as Chief Manager, broke the news to Baranov
on January 11, 1818. The Suvorov was held back until
the 14th, so she could convey the news to the Main
Office.

The commissioner aboard the Kutuzov [K. T.
Khlebnikov] was appointed Office Manager to take over
the funds from Baranov. This worthy old man had no one
at that time to whom he could entrust the rich storehouses. He therefore sent employees to relinquish them
in his place, but he handed over personally the most
important fur goods.

The receipt of stores and inventory from Baranov and
the preparation of accounts lasted until September. In
the interval the new Chief Manager, wishing to implement
the late N. P. Rezanov's plan, which had been approved
by the Main Office, persuaded the promyshlenniks to
relinquish the old method of payment by shares in kind,
and to accept a monetary basis of payment. Concurrently
the Company agreed to supply them with provisions each
month. This new responsibility forced him to set off
for California aboard the Kutuzov. He left Sitka on
June 22 and returned on October 3 with 15,000 puds of
various types of grain and a large quantity of other
supplies.

The colonies were now well provisioned, and Hagemeister arranged to return to Russia himself and to
hand over the duties of Chief Manager to Lieutenant
Ianovskii, who could be relied upon in all things,
including the administration of the colonies – and he
justified this faith.

The capital turned over at Sitka from Baranov's
administration equalled two and a half million rubles.
It included inventory worth 900,000 rubles, and furs
apart from those sent on the Suvorov, approximating
200,000 rubles at colonial prices, but there were only

three sailing vessels fit for use: the ship <u>Otkrytie</u>, the brig <u>Il'mena</u>, and the schooner <u>Chirikov</u>. The sloop <u>Konstantin</u> had now grown old and the two unseaworthy craft, the <u>Zlatoust'</u> and <u>Platov</u> were valueless. The ships' commanders were Lieutenant Podushkin and the foreigners Benzeman, Young, and the sickly Abram Jones.

The 72 year old Baranov wished only peace for himself, but he hesitated in choosing a place to pass his last days when he felt his end not far off. Habit, which acts upon people as it acts upon Nature, inclined him to remain in the colonies and settle in Kad'iak. But the constant isolation, unremitting boredom and damp climate of the place had already taken effect on him. Family ties demanded their due and he had on occasion thought of finishing his days in Izhiga with his brother, his only remaining relative in Russia. At times he thought of moving to the Sandwich Islands and ending his days in the charming valleys of this part of Australia [i.e. the South Seas] presented him by his old friend King Kamehameha, and which even after the Sheffer episode were considered Baranov's property. The worthy and respected V. M. Golovnin, who was in Sitka on the sloop <u>Kamchatka,</u> advised him to return to Russia where the members of the Russian-American Company, obligated to him more than anyone else as the developer of the colonies as they now were, would undoubtedly undertake to provide him with all the perquisites of a peaceful and pleasant life. While there he could still benefit the Company through his knowledge of colonial affairs and his advice.

These proposals were convincing and Baranov decided, not without regret, to leave the places where for 28 years he had labored constantly and ceaselessly, often in anguish and need, and seldom in comfort and plenty. Not without tears did he part from his former employees and colleagues, who had so often willingly shared his labors and hardships, and followed him boldly into danger.

Many of his colleagues were grey haired and aged
like himself. They who had shared his adventures and
campaigns now sobbed like children as they parted forever with their beloved leader. Many of those who now
surrounded him had grown up under his administration.
He was godfather to many, and had taught most of the
younger ones. He had been above all a benefactor, and
now, bidding farewell, he left them all forever. Even
the Kolosh who had trembled before him, but respected
his bold and decisive spirit, parted from him with a
strange mixture of joy and sadness. The famed toen
Kotleian, respected by Baranov for his intelligence
and bravery, and who had harmed Baranov more than anyone
by destroying the fort – even he appeared before him,
and they made their peace. Baranov bore witness to his
successor concerning this man's intelligence and ability.
As they bade farewell, he beseeched his successor to
send him news of even the smallest events in the
colonies, saying that this would bring him joy in the
turbulent world outside.

On November 27 the Kutuzov left Sitka. Baranov's
colleague Lieutenant Podushkin travelled with him as
did his chief clerk and three servants.

On December 23 they approached the Sandwich Islands,
but their Captain did not land there, but headed for
Manila. Contrary winds prevented them from reaching
port, and for fresh supplies they put in at Umata
harbor on the island of Guam on January 28, 1819. They
spent three days there and then sailed on to Batavia,
where they arrived March 7 and remained for 36 days.

It is well known that the climate in Batavia is
harmful for Europeans, particularly the aged, but even
more apt to be fatal for the failing, like Baranov.
For his whole stay in Batavia he lived on shore in an
inn, and the mortal poison of the climate infected him.
He had already had bouts of illness when they left
Batavia on the 12th. In the Straits of Sunda on April
16 1819, the productive and celebrated life of this

outstanding man ended. He died who was to remain unforgettable for the Russian-American Company--the first Manager of its colonies. The following day, off Prince Island, a funeral service was held and his body was lowered over the side. The waters of the Indian Ocean closed forever over the last earthly remains of Aleksandr Andreevich Baranov.

CONCLUSION

In this biography we have followed Baranov's path,
with fair attention to details which do not require
special explanation. We have seen how, on his arrival
in America, he found just one colony, in Kad'iak. Here,
and on the islands nearby, the stocks of sea otters, on
which the Company's well-being depended, and from which
its riches were drawn, were almost exhausted. Gradually,
with time, he brought to his way of thinking the savage
inhabitants of the Alaska Peninsula and of part of the
mainland of North America, as far as Lake Iliamna. From
Lebedev-Lastochkin's company he took over the area
around Kenai Bay and occupied the whole of Chugatsk Bay
to the mouth of the Copper River, along whose course
many settlements were established.

Moving further southeast he established settlements
at Mt. St. Elias, then in Yakutat, and finally occupied
the broad island of Sitka, which was separated from the
mainland by a strait. The Main Office of the Company
renamed this island Baranov Island in recognition of his
services, and it bears this name on Russian maps. There,
a port was constructed in the good harbor of Novo-
Arkhangel'sk - and is to this day the administrative
center of the colonies. This port is situated at
Latitude 57°3' N. and Longitude 135°33' W. Consequently,
Russian territories were extended from Kad'iak some 16 ,
or 550 miles, eastward.

With the merging of the Shelikhov and Irkutsk
Companies all of the Aleutian and Pribylov Islands were
placed under Baranov's jurisdiction except for the
Andreianov group, which continued to be administered
from the Company office in Okhotsk. The spread of
colonies of the Russian-American Company ceased with the

establishment of the Ross fort on New Albion. Thus,
after taking over in 1791 the small artel in Three
Saints Harbor on Kad'iak Island, in 1818 Baranov left
the main factory at Sitka and permanent branches at
Kad'iak, Unalashka and Ross with separate hunting posts
on the Pribylov Islands, and in Kenai Bay and Chugatsk
Bay.

Here, by the way, it seems apposite to introduce
some remarks about our colonies in Northwest America,
which also have a bearing on Baranov.

There were and still are people, worthy of respect,
who ask what good it does for Russia to occupy the
Northwest Coast of America, especially when the mainten-
ance of colonies there involves considerable expense.
To these people it can quite boldly be replied: there
are and must be advantages, on one condition--that we
know how to exploit them. They must be developed
through active and intelligent effort, without which
nothing can be achieved. If not Russia then certainly
England, or the United States of America would have
occupied those coasts long ago. Baranov lacked the
strength; and the Americans decided only belatedly to
settle the Columbia River, which the British subsequently forced them to give up. Later when the Con-
vention was concluded with Russia in 1824, they moved
right up to our territory, to the very border at 54°30'
and fortified Observatory Inlet (called Naz in the
Kolosh language). As a result, the English value these
areas highly and hope to profit from them.

It seems that Baranov, on the evidence he had available moved firmly in the right direction and achieved
a measure of success, but it turned out to be both insufficient and incomplete. In his haste to occupy and
settle the coastal strips, since they were the most
easily accessible, he missed the opportunity to
establish firm bases in the hinterland, where there
could have been a profitable trade in skins and furs of
river beaver, otters, sables, bears, and so forth. The

British seized on this, and the Company's territory was
restricted to a strip ten leagues deep from the coast.
In the course of time when Russia, marching forward with
giant steps on the path to enlightenment, will be
striving to enrich and expand the prosperity of the
Empire, then a main branch of our popular riches--mer-
chant navigation--will spread and flourish, and we, like
other trading nations, will cross the distant seas in
our own ships built and directed by our own merchants
and workers. Only then will the value of such places be
realized, where now so little attention is directed,
and our descendants, perhaps, will say how far-sighted
we were.

There is another objection: what is the use if the
local population are disobedient and hostile? I reply:
they may be so now, but if we can only be patient and
careful, the time will come of itself, when through
trade and imitation of our habits, through social mixing
as a result of education and intermarriage, and through
the almighty action of God's Mercy, attitudes will
soften.

From these reasons, their culture will slowly but
surely come up to the desired standard. And, if not we,
then our descendants, will have a good inheritance in
America.

The reproof is also made that the population of
Kad'iak has decreased--but any who criticize should re-
call that in none of the European colonies in the New
World has the original population increased or remained
intact and unharmed. For that they will have to blame
Columbus and the inventive minds of his followers, and
then navigation, trade and enlightenment. It is these
which have either directly or indirectly in these newly
discovered countries spread diseases hitherto unknown
amongst the savages, together with new needs, whims, and
vices. The natives have decreased in numbers for one
or another of these reasons.

Shelikhov, to increase his own fame, over-estimated the number of subject peoples on Kad'iak as 50,000 souls. This exaggeration was spread abroad and many believed Shelikhov's word without correction, witnesses or evidence, and angrily attacked the innocent Baranov when the true figure turned out to be only 6,000. Langsdorf, considering this matter, blames Baranov, alleging that the majority of Aleuts were killed in sea otter hunting by baidarka.[64] A detailed account is given above of where and how this happened, and the number of those who died at different times does not exceed 500. No single native of Kad'iak has ever charged Baranov with destroying the original inhabitants of their island. They themselves see that their numbers have decreased, but they ascribe it to disease, and this is the only, the most just, and for us the almost inevitable reason for the diminution in population. Its effects may well continue to be felt until intermixing brings the temperament [i.e., ability to thrive] of succeeding generations up to that of their masters.

Let us take as an example Kamchatka, where there was no Baranov and there were no hunting expeditions. At the time of first settlement there were more than 10,000 native inhabitants. The region was plagued by smallpox in 1768 and 1769; in all, 5,440 people died and 3,791 remained. A contagious rotting fever, introduced by the Kamchatka battalion in 1800, destroyed almost half the population. The Kamchadals and Koriaks continue to be decimated by a disease which, because of the similarity of attacks, some call venereal. It is ascribed, perhaps wrongly, to the Russians there, but both its nature and its origins are still uncertain. In the spring of 1827, in Izhiga and Okhotsk, there was a dangerous and fatal outbreak of infection which carried off more natives than visitors. In our colonies there were similar outbreaks in 1806, 1808, 1819 and 1824, and these took many lives.

Let us take another, more recent example, not in

our territories. In the areas around the Columbia River
occupied by the British, the local population was dense
up until 1830. Then a persistent rotting fever appeared,
and four-fifths of the inhabitants died. Of course,
there were epidemics among them before the Europeans
came, but rarely; there remains no history of them, nor
memorials or legends. Vancouver found in the Port Discovery area (Latitude 48°7' and Longitude 237°20') a
huge quantity of skulls and other human bones strewn
about so widely that it seemed to him to have been a
mass grave. He could discover no cause for this havoc,
but justly concluded that it was the result of some
epidemic disease.[65]

In California catarrh and measles often appeared,
the latter called there sarampion. Both these diseases
were fatal for the natives. They spread without contact, and were perhaps air borne to the north, where
they did similar damage. In Kad'iak, isolated from the
mainland, epidemic diseases often appeared which, did
not harm the Russians, but were fatal for the natives.
At other times and other places, deep-rooted super-
stition would have it that the Russians were spreading
diseases among the natives, but, thanks to enlightenment about this, such tales were unheard of in our
colonies.

Ukamok Island lies far from the others and is
visited only once a year, but in winter during the
epidemic in Kad'iak, when there was no contact with the
Ukamok people, the same disease appeared, with the same
fatal effects. The same, to all intents, could be said
of the cholera which more recently affected the
Europeans also.

Perhaps through the unseen paths of Providence all
the indigenous peoples of the New World will gradually
disappear or mix in with the new arrivals, but the
places where they lived will not remain empty.

Thus it would be futile to blame Baranov for having
decimated the population and to accuse him of

unrestricted and cruel expansion of our domain in northwest America. He is not guilty of the first, and deserves the Company's undying gratitude and the Fatherland's recognition for the reputation gained in
acquiring new lands and peoples. The honors which he
did not claim and did not seek for himself, but which he
deserved through his noble qualities, already justify
him in the eyes of his contemporaries. Posterity, as
it examines his dealings and his heroic deeds and
weighs the strengths and weaknesses he showed while
carrying out his achievements, will doubtless render him
the just and due praise which he deserves.

If brave Ermak and Shelikhov are renowned, then
Baranov, of course, will not be less so. He retained
and strengthened Shelikhov's territories, and as far as
possible enlightened and educated the people there entrusted to him. Shelikhov, it could be said, only
initiated his own proposals; but Baranov finished and
brought them to fruition. We all know that it is easier
to propose than to dispose. Apart from this, he himself
made further and greater settlements than Shelikhov ever
dreamt of.

Without laboring the question of the capital held by
Shelikhov's Company, it became evident after his death,
when the companies amalgamated in 1796, that the total
assets were 724,000 rubles, which by 1799 had grown to
1,298,000 rubles, and the complete Company turnover at
that time stood at 2,588,000 rubles. This was the
situation at the beginning of Baranov's administration,
but before he was replaced in 1816, the Company capital
reached 4,800,000 rubles, and its complete turnover was
just under 7,000,000 rubles. In the colonies alone the
physical assets, including goods, munitions, raw
materials, ships, buildings, mills and so forth, turned
over by Baranov to the Company came to 2,500,000 rubles.

The Company's huge returns to Russia included furs,
and, according to one reliable estimate by the Main
Office, in the period from 1806 to 1818 alone some 15

million rubles entered Russia this way, while at the
same time only 2,800,000 rubles left Russia for America.
This difference was because Baranov, without demanding
imports, bartered goods for goods and traded with the
foreigners. In this way he put into the storehouses in
Kad'iak and Sitka up to 5,000 sea otters, 4,000 beaver
tails, 10,000 river beavers and up to 400,000 fur seals,
worth in all about 1,200,000 rubles. Apart from goods
and supplies five ships were bartered for this, the
Juno, Kad'iak, Il'mena, Bering, and Amethyst.

    There are numerous examples of this kind to indicate
Baranov's painstaking, unselfish, and fruitful care for
the Company's interests. Under his administration the
Company's assets (apart from expenses and dividends paid
on shares) doubled, but if his sound undertakings had
succeeded as planned, then certainly the real increase
is more than double. One must remember the misfortunes
and disasters which repeatedly blocked his path: the
wreck of the Phoenix with her cargo from Okhotsk, and
the loss of all on board; the wreck of the cutter Orel,
of the brig Sitka, the ship Juno, of the brigs
Elisaveta, Aleksandr and Maria; of the ships Neva and
Bering with their rich cargoes of sea otter furs and
Russian goods; the wreck of the Eclipse with her cargo
of wares from Canton; the destruction of the settlements
in Sitka and Yakutat, and finally the fiery Sheffer's
Sandwich Island fiasco. These losses approximately
equalled the Company's actual assets, but the loss of
men and potentials was beyond measure.

    During Baranov's administration the Company's
affairs sharply improved, gained successful momentum,
and were established on a basis of good repute, trust
and respect. After His Gracious Majesty turned his
attention to the matter, the Company was awarded a flag
bearing the Imperial crest; this has flown with honor
over vessels which have sailed several times around the
globe.

    For his services, Baranov was brought to the

attention of the Emperors Paul and Alexander. From the
former he received a gold medal, and by the latter he
was appointed direct to the rank of Collegiate
Councillor with the order of St. Anna, 2nd Class.

The worthy shareholders of the Russian-American
Company consistently respected and supported his
instructions. The Company's accredited representative
Actual Chamberlain N. P. Rezanov, writing to Khvostov,
refers to Baranov's noble feelings and love for his
Fatherland. He says of him: "In the Manager of these
areas, we see an example of eagerness and energy at
which posterity will some day wonder more than we."
But the strongest proof of Baranov's value to the
Company is contained in the words of the highly respected Director of the Main Office who, at the Company
shareholders meeting in 1822, expressed himself thus:
"Baranov alone is responsible for building up new
capital for the Company!" In these few but expressive
words rests a shining and firm memorial to him.

Foreigners trading along the Northwest Coast of
America looked upon Baranov's labors and achievements
with amazement and respect, and watched enviously the
spread of our possessions. At a session of the United
States Congress in January, 1821, a committee memorandum
was read concerning our colonies, in which the fortification of Ross and Sitka, amongst other things, was
discussed:

> A people who are in a condition to undertake
> journeys, often through barely passable mountains
> and across ice-filled seas during such storms and
> blizzards that it is impossible to see more than
> a few paces ahead, naturally knows the full
> importance and value of trade, for which reason
> they embark upon such lengthy wanderings. In
> order to never be deprived of means achieved at
> such cost and by such sacrifice and to exploit
> to the full their advantages, Russia has con-
> sidered it necessary to occupy one of the Sand-
> wich Islands and to take other action.[66]

In his letters from Sitka to St. Petersburg, Actual

Chamberlain N. P. Rezanov explains:

>   We are all living here in very cramped
> conditions, but worse than anyone lives the man
> who is responsible for gaining us these terri-
> tories. He lives in a kind of plank lean-to so
> full of damp that every day mould has to be
> wiped off, and during the local heavy rains it
> leaks like a sieve. What a man! He worries
> only about the comfort of others, but so
> neglects his own comfort that one day I found
> his bed awash and asked if the weather-boarding
> had split from the wall beside his bed. "No,"
> he replied quietly, "plainly it leaks through
> from the square," and he continued about his
> business. I tell you, my dear Sirs, that Bara-
> nov is an original and happy product of Nature.
> His name is renowned all along the West coast
> right down to California. The Bostonians res-
> pect and admire him, while the native peoples
> fear him, and, even from remote parts, send him
> offers of friendship. This spring the famous
> toen Kau from Kaigan sent his son on a Boston
> ship to behold Baranov and make his acquaintance.
> I confess to you that this man fascinates me.
> The important consequences of his acquisitions
> will soon make him better appreciated in Russia,
> and I think his vital characteristics will
> please his fellow-countrymen who are not
> affected by slavish imitation of foreign models,
> and who appreciate the deeds of true Russians
> in their rightful perspective. That is, those
> who acknowledge his achievements and weigh them
> impartially, against those failings and weak-
> nesses peculiar to man which result from faults
> in upbringing or long ingrained habits.[67]

Lieutenant of the Fleet Gavrila Ivanovich Davydov,
inseparable companion of the famous Khvostov, gives a
lively and impartial picture of Baranov in the notes on
his voyages of 1802:

>   I cannot look upon this man without a certain
> respect; a man who has devoted his life improving
> conditions in the field of trade. He has now
> been living in America for 12 long years, with
> savage and coarse peoples; surrounded by constant
> danger, struggling with the innate immorality of
> the local Russians, with endless work, faced by
> all the basic needs, including hunger itself.
> This he has done with almost no one who could
> match his energy, in spite of the lack of the
> means to expand trade, and of the vengefulness
> of some peoples, and of opposition to his
> attempts to ease the burden of others, enslaved

by the Russian-American Company. He seems to
have been completely unaided, left on his own
to seek his own survival and that of the
institutions in America. All these tasks,
obstacles, sorrows, needs, and failures have
not weakened this splendid man's spirit,
although they have naturally darkened his
outlook a little. Baranov is not very talk-
ative; he is dry, until you know him closely.
But he always makes his points with fervor,
and especially about matters with which he is
currently occupied. It is not easy to know
him well, but he will do anything for his
friends. He loves to entertain foreigners,
sharing everything he has, and always gladly
helps the poor. Complete disinterestedness is
not his only virtue. He is not only in-
different to amassing a fortune, but even
shares what he has with needy friends. His
steadiness of spirit and constant presence of
mind have made savages respect him, without
loving him. Baranov's fame resounds amongst
these barbarians who inhabit the Northwest
Coast of America as far south as the Straits
of Juan de Fuca. Even those living far away
sometimes travel specially to see him, and
they wonder that such great deeds should be
accomplished by such a small man. Baranov is
below average height, fair-haired, and thickset. His face is deeply lined by his many
worries and affairs, even though he is now
only 56.

This is how a young, educated observer describes him,
one who lived with him in a small group for eight months,
and must know the truth. He had no need to flatter him.
In faithfully describing the life style of the natives,
he openly presented all his affairs and instructions,
which sometimes, in their details showed mistakes and   mis
omissions. These might seem ill-conceived to those not
knowing local conditions and former practices. Many
superficial observers, where they see no good, see evil.
But it is always wise to consider the end and the means,
and the conclusion should be drawn that he did only what
had to be done because of the circumstances. Rulings
which from outside might seem to be malpractice, were
the result of practical realities.

Baranov has been accused in regard to his economic
measures: but if we turn to the first period of the

administration we will see that, left to his own
devices, beyond the Russian borders, on uninhabited
islands, or in the forests of America, he had to find
his own ingenious ways to support honorably the territories he had acquired, and not to lose but to develop
the fur trade there. Bearing all this in mind, he
brought peace, contentment, and even plenty, to the
peoples entrusted to his administration. To the Company
he brought much profit and advantage. One might have
expected that public attention would be turned on the
Company's affairs, and that even greater efforts on his
part would have been encouraged.

For we all know that the public, and especially the
trading community, looks only for successes and judges
the entrepreneurs' character by his profits, and pays
him their due. They will not analyse the reasons for
decline in trade, falling profits, or failing business.

From the very outset the Company never put into the
colonies sufficient wares to barter with the savages,
or even pay them. For example, in 1802, Khvostov on
the brig <u>Elisaveta</u> delivered 20,000 rubles worth of
various articles, many of them unnecessary. But the
need to pay the Aleuts for their hunting, then rich,
required 150,000 rubles. Because Baranov was in
financial straits he had to extract articles for payment from local produce. He set the Aleuts to catching
birds and marmots, making parkas from the skins, and
used these to pay the Aleuts for work, hunting and so
forth. These are the details on which Baranov's vili-
fiers base their evidence. But is he at fault for
this? He said nothing about the periods of inattention
or failure by the Company to acknowledge his demands.
It is clear apart from paying for work and hunting, one
of the Chief Manager's obligations is to care for the
upkeep and feeding of all the inhabitants, Russians and
natives. The natives, from innate idleness and carelessness, never bothered about the future. But Baranov's good and sympathetic heart was moved for them.

He sympathized when there were no fish to be caught, no whales to be harpooned, no seals, and so on. He spent sleepless nights when storms delayed the arrival of expected supply ships, or when they foundered and upset all his plans for the general good. It is said that whenever a vessel was wrecked off the coast of Kamchatka, he was on the Northwest Coast of America sick at heart, with no relief for his dark forebodings. But how his heart must have ached when batches of bad news suddenly arrived together, like the loss of the settlement in Sitka and the annihilation of the hunting party; or the foundering of ships with rich cargoes, cargoes on which they had depended for survival and future profits? Naturally, not having been in similar circumstances, it is not easy to imagine the sorrow and devastating grief such news could bring; but I will call to witness Baranov's worthy successors, convinced that they, knowing local conditions and experiencing some of the same worries and heartaches, see premature grey hairs and wrinkles - true signs of nervous exhaustion and anxiety. They will give their predecessor's trials their true value. I have had the honor to hear how one of them, on learning how Baranov, suddenly receiving the news of the wreck of the _Elisaveta_, of the swallowing up by the sea of six baidaras and Dem'ianenkov's party, and of the destruction of the fort at Yakutat, suddenly exclaimed with heartfelt sympathy: "My God! How could he bear such misfortunes?"

Apart from caring for the economy, hunting and trade, Baranov did not neglect his task of educating the young people born in the colonies. In his time Sitka had a school which taught reading and arithmetic. Under his guidance, accounting courses were later provided, while other pupils became shipmasters' mates, others learnt trades, and still others were sent to Petersburg for further education. Three were sent on the _Neva_ and three more on the _Suvorov_ and the _Borodino_. Of these latter two, A. Kashevarov returned to the colonies as an

ensign of the Navigator's Corps, while Nedomolvin and
Terent'ev returned as armory and navigation masters.
Baranov sent one of the better Kolosh, toen Naushket's
brother, to Petersburg for training, accompanied by
several Kolosh commoners. But none of them, unfortun-
ately, returned to give their fellow tribesmen reliable
information about European civilization and the might of
Russia. On Kad'iak an institution was set up to care
for the daughters of the poor, but when Baranov was
away this institution never achieved its aims. For these
charitable institutions Baranov sacrificed five of his
own shares.

Let us say a little more about his nature and character. Baranov never dreamt of amassing wealth. As the
proverb says: death showed life, and justified him in
face of unjust and insulting suspicions. It was said
that he had considerable sums deposited in foreign banks.
Without touching anyone else's property he always lived
by his own earnings. Shelikhov had issued him with ten
shares, but when Shelikhov's Company merged with the
Irkutsk one this was raised to 20 for administering the
colonies. Of these, he shared five each with his
colleagues Kuskov and Banner, who were on low salaries
which the shareholders felt, in the circumstances then,
could not be increased, nor could any aid be given from
the total fur catch. He recognized his colleagues'
needs, and gave them half his pay, without informing the
Company. Banner and Kuskov fully appreciated this
generosity, and the former, deploring his situation,
wrote to one of the Directors, saying; "Although it is
shameful for Kuskov and me to take Baranov's shares,
need forces us to it." Further on, discussing the
reasons for their meager standard of living, he writes
that he has long wanted to complain about the situation,
"but only Aleksandr Andreevich's generosity held back my
hand and sealed my lips."

Baranov helped not only his friends who were poor
but even his enemies who were in distress. There are

still many people in the colonies who received his bene-
factions. Many had a chance to return home with his
aid. Many of his juniors who were under scrutiny had
their loads lightened, and were shielded by him. In
addition to all this, he sent back to Russia considerable
sums as presents and likewise, and in this way helped
many of his friends who were, by ill chance out of work
or in need. Amongst these was Koch, who was for several
years under investigation, with no work or means of
support. Baranov, knowing his situation, and the large
family he had to support, sent him money regularly.

By generously rewarding the services of his employees
and helping his friends out of his own pocket, it could
be said that Baranov was almost mean with Company property. He believed he had no right to personally dispose of it, without the Company's approval, and benefit.
When the Company was granted privileges and Imperial
patronage, he gave from his own funds, as we have seen,
thousands of rubles. But of Company property, on that
triumphal day of joy, he ordered only one sheep to be
slaughtered, an old one at that. This proves again how
much care and joy he had in the breeding of cattle in
the colonies. It must be added that he was responsible
for introducing cattle to the Aleutian Islands. When
he gave up the administration there were already 300
head of horned cattle on Kad'iak alone. At Ross, from
its inception to about 1818, there were 60 cows, 160
sheep, 10 horses and many pigs. From Kad'iak cattle
were sent to Unalashka, Unga, to some settlements in
Alaska, and to the fort at Nikolaevsk. In Sitka there
were about 10 cows which provided milk for the sick and
for the officials--it was difficult to keep more there
through lack of fodder.

Davydov noted that selflessness was not his only
virtue, and points to his generosity. To this I must
add that his generous spirit was exceeded only by
generosity of heart. He was quick to forgive personal
wrongs. One of many examples, from his business

activity, well illustrates this. In November, 1800,
some escaped Aleuts were captured and brought to Kad'iak
for inspection. On arrival, they were taken straight to
Baranov, and it was by chance discovered that they had
daggers concealed under their clothing. When asked why,
they confessed that if Baranov had ordered corporal
punishment, they were going to strike him down and then
kill themselves. Baranov merely lectured them for
running away, but their evil design, as he put it, "he
left God to judge." He knew from experience that for
the Aleuts nothing is more shameful than corporal punishment. To escape it, guilty persons had often committed
suicide. Knowing this, he usually punished the Aleuts
who came before him with shame, or by making them work
for a stipulated period. Davydov remarks that, "the
Koniagas consider corporal punishment a great dishonor"
- and points out several occasions of ferocity.[69]

I shall produce one more example which shows the
respect with which he was held. During his stay in
Chugatsk Bay in 1792, as previously related, he came
upon an East-Indiaman whose Captain came to like Baranov
and as proof of his friendship presented him with his
own Bengal Indian slave, Richard. This Indian, who was
constantly at Baranov's side, and at sea filled the post
of boatswain, learned to speak good Russian, and, during
Baranov's visit to Sitka, in 1800, served as his interpreter in discussions with foreign sea captains. Baranov, respecting his services, rewarded him and allowed
him to go as he pleased on the ships which were then
visiting Sitka. This circumstance was all the more
remarkable, since Baranov knew no foreign languages, and
was thus dependent on him, and could have required him to
stay as long as he liked.

It has been said above that Baranov saw this vessel
in Chugatsk Bay, outside the area of the settlement, and
among savage and hostile peoples. This prompted one
partner to suggest that they might seize the ship and
throw the blame onto the natives: Baranov answered this

remark with disgust: "How could you think that I would
break the sacred laws of hospitality and stain these
shores with the blood of innocent visitors, leaving on
myself the irremovable blot of treachery?"[70]

An equally important example of probity stands in
Baranov's letter to Larionov of July 1, 1802, in which
he writes:

> after the wreck of the Orel, the cabin-trunk
> of the drowned administrator Polomoshnoi,
> with his written effects, was dried out, sealed,
> and delivered here. I did not want to break the
> seal without a witness, or examine the contents,
> which, because of the deceased's hostile atti-
> tude I suspected might contain information
> against me.

The misfortunes and disasters which often befell and
tortured Baranov; the boredom of loneliness; the constant isolation from civilized society, and even written
contact with it only once a year; the promyshlenniks from
the common folk who surrounded and lived with him; the
coarseness of some of his foreign visitors--all this
left on him traces of moroseness and unsociability,
which might seem to the passing visitor from educated
society to be even severity or fierceness. But those
who knew him better thought otherwise--just as Davydov
introduced us to him. Normally, Baranov was not talk-
ative, and did not overflow with effusive greetings; he
was, so to speak, thrifty with his friendships; but what
he said was wise and he sometimes liked to interject a
few jokes. His statements were well thought out, and
his undertaking were always directed as far as possible
to the profit and advantage of the Company, at whose
service he had placed the whole of his being.

On his replacement some worthy, knowledgeable and
educated men were sent to the colonies, amongst them
Messrs. Etholen and Shmit. In the course of one
friendly and frank conversation, of open-hearted sailors'
talk, when Ianovskii was host, Baranov said, through
tears: "If only the Main Office could have sent me men

like yourselves earlier, then I would very likely have
had more success, and I would have found it pleasant to
pass the time in their company!"

He was already over 70 when I saw him, but even then
his eyes still shone with a lively and penetrating gaze.
He had a full face, lined with the marks of age; his
cheeks were ruddy, but touched already with pallor. He
was bald, and so he wore a wig, held in place by a black
band under his chin. Vasilii Mikhailovich Golovnin,
respected and much esteemed by Baranov, wishing to preserve his image for posterity, asked him to let the
artist Tikhanov do a portrait. He was asked to remove
his wig and his bare head conveyed special importance
to his expressive face.

Baranov's speech was slow and measured, with no
exclamations or gesticulations. He had no love of
fashion, and preferred the uniform he had worn when
promoted (1805), to anything new, regardless of the fact
that in 14 years, changing fashions had made it out-
moded. Of thickset build, he was said in his prime to
have been upright, strong and agile; he walked with a
quiet tread. Among his good qualities it must be re-
corded that he did not like games of any sort (apart
from billiards), and playing for money even less so. No
one dared bring cards into the colonies. He feared them
like a contagious disease which could easily spread and
might never be eradicated. He read much, and most of
the fictional and historical works produced by Russian
belle lettres to 1803 were to be found in the colonies;
in that year lovers of enlightenment had dispatched
them aboard the ship Nadezhda. In America he had a son,
Antipatr, and a daughter by an American native girl.
V. M. Golovnin took his son to Russia aboard the sloop
Kamchatka. Shortly after arrival in Petersburg Antipatr
died and the daughter, having now married, also died
shortly after arrival in Russia. Her children, and
Aleksandr Andreevich's grandchildren by his first

daughter, who had remained in Russia, became heirs to a small estate that was nothing to boast about.

The End

GLOSSARY

artel (Russian)--a work crew, as a large group of hunters.

baidarshchik (R.)--head of a work crew and of the territory in which it operates.

prikashchik (R.)--agent or supercargo.

promyshlennik--Russian fur trapper and trader.

Creole--a person of Russian and Alaska native parentage.

Kolosh--Russian name for Tlingit Indians.

archimandrite--superior of a monastery or convent in the Greek Church.

hieromonk--a monk who is also a priest.

toen (or toion)--Russian term for native chieftain, carried to Alaska from Siberia.

baidara (R.)--a skin boat, holding 20-25 people.

baidarka (R.)--an Eskimo or Aleut kayak, holding one, two or three persons.

sazhen (R.)--7 feet.

toise--old French measure, of about 6 feet.

verst (R.)--0.6629 mile or 1.067 kilometers.

fanega--a dry measure in Spain (1.58 bu.) and Spanish America (varies).

pud, or pood (R.)--36.11 pounds avoirdupois.

ruble (R.)-- U.S. $0.50.

kopek (R.)--U.S. ½ cent, or 1/100 ruble.

piaster--a Spanish peso or dollar of the early nineteenth century, equal to about U.S. $1.00 of the time.

NOTES

Notes, or portions of notes preceded by an asterisk (*) have been added. Source information in Khlebnikov's notes has been expanded in some cases, or English versions, where available, substituted for Russian sources.

*[1] See P. A. Tikhmenev, Istoricheskoe obozrenie obrazovaniia Rossiisko-Amerikanskoi kompanii i deistvii ee do nastoiashchego vremeni, vols. I-II, St. P., 1861, 1863. I, pp. 32-33, for some of provisions of agreement between Shelikhov and Baranov, concluded at Okhotsk August 18, 1790, the day before Baranov sailed.
Tikhmenev, Chap. I, note 8, distinguishes between valovoi (investment) and sukhovye (donative) shares. The former were held by direct participants in the voyage, either the owner or the promyshlenniks. The latter were given to the church or to a sea captain or a company director for his services, or they were assigned to persons able to influence the course of the undertaking.

[2] [Dmitrii Ivanovich] Bocharov, had been in Kamchatka in 1771 during Beniowski's revolt, was taken prisoner by him and conveyed to France. Thence, through the good offices of the Russian ambassador he was transferred to St. Petersburg and from there sent to Okhotsk at the behest of the Empress. He had gained a consummate knowledge of seamanship during his wanderings half way around the world.

[3] After long use in water, skins (laftak) begin to rot.

*[4] See "Map of Alaska Peninsula prepared by Navigator Bocharov in November 1791," in A. V. Efimov, Atlas geograficheskikh otkrytii v Sibiri i v Severo-Zapadnoi Amerike XVII-XVIII vv. Moscow, 1964. Map 180, and p. 117.

*[5] Adam J. VonKrusenstern. Voyage round the world in the years 1803, 1804, 1805, and 1806. Translated from the original German. London, 1813, and Amsterdam/New York, 1968, 2 v. I, p. xx.

[6] Evstrat Ivanovich Delarov, a native of Peloponnesus, traded in Moscow and joined the Company for trade in America. He administered the employees there and

commanded ships. He was later a Director of the
Russian-American Company and a Commercial Councilor.

[7]A baidara holds 20-25 people. (*) This seems to be
a paraphrase from a letter, Baranov to Shelikhov, from
Chugach Bay, July 24, 1793, in Tikhmenev, II, Appendix,
pp. 37-38; see also narrative in Tikhmenev, I, p. 34.

[8]See George Vancouver, A voyage of discovery to the
North Pacific Ocean...in the years 1790, 1791, 1792,
1793, 1794, and 1795... London, 1793, 3 vols. III,
pp. 114 ff.

*[9]A misstatement. Vancouver never met Baranov,
though he refers to him in his Vol. 3, pp. 127, 143,
144, 172-173. In Tikhmenev, I, p. 42, Baranov writes
Shelikhov: "Circumstances prevented me from seeing
them, although they invited me and waited several days
around Kenai Bay. My subordinates, however, showed
them all hospitality." Presumably Baranov avoided
meeting the English captain, since at that time it was
thought his expedition was intended to discover to what
limits the Russians wished to extend their territory
along the American coast.

[10]List of people making up the religious mission:
1. Archimandrite Ioasaf...drowned on the Phoenix in 1799.
2. Hieromonk Juvenal ...killed by savages in North America.
3. Hieromonk Makarii ...sent in 1795, then left of his
   own will for Okhotsk.
4. Hieromonk Afanasii...sent to Irkutsk in 1825.
5. Hierodeacon Stefan...drowned in retinue of the Arch-
   bishop.
6. Hierodeacon Nektarii...sent to Irkutsk by Gedeon
   in 1807.
7. Monk German...still alive.
8. Monk Ioasaf...died on Kad'iak in 1823.

[11]A suloi is a conflict between two opposing
currents or a strong current with wind giving rise to
great waves. The stronger the current and the wind, the
more violent the suloi.

*[12]See letter, Baranov to Shelikhov and Polevoi, from
Pavlovsk Harbor, May 20, 1795, Tikhmenev, II, Appendix,
p. 88.

[13]See Shelikhov's Voyages, part II.

*[14]Khlebnikov gives a false picture of harmony be-
tween Baranov and the Archimandrite; they were at odds
almost constantly.

[15]Ivan Aleksandrovich Kuskov, a merchant from
Tot'ma, went to America with Baranov as a prikashchik;
he was soon selected by Baranov as an assistant and was

used in all the most important undertakings; his ardent execution of these were later rewarded with a gold medal, and he was promoted to Commercial Councilor. He left the Company's service in 1821, returned to Russia via Okhotsk in 1822, and died in Tot'ma in 1823.

[16]See Journey of Captain Sarychev, Part II, pp. 55-56.

[17]For a description of the [Zosima and Savatiia's] remarkable voyage see the travels of Lieutenant Davydov and V. I. Berkh's history of the Aleutian Islands.

*[18]See Tikhmenev, II, Appendix, pp. 148-149. From letter, Baranov to Larionov, from Kad'iak Island, July 24, 1800. Up to this point, Tikhmenev's is the better version in that Khlebnikov's has been paraphrased and corrected, but from this point the rest of the passage given by Khlebnikov is omitted by Tikhmenev.

*[19]See letter, Baranov to Larionov, July 24, 1800, in Tikhmenev, II, Appendix, p. 139, and letter, Baranov to Skipper Talin, May, 1799, in Tikhmenev, II, Appendix, pp. 125-130.

*[20]Cf. Donald J. Orth, Dictionary of Alaska Place Names, Washington, D. C., 1967, p. 722.

*[21]See letter, Baranov to Larionov, July 24, 1800, p. 139, Tikhmenev, II, Appendix, p. 142.

*[22]Ibid., p. 144.

*[23]Ibid., p. 146.

*[24]Ibid., p. 146.

[25]See Vancouver, II, p. 364.

*[26]See Instruction, Baranov to Medvednikov (left to manage affairs at Novo-Arkhangel'sk) about the need to strengthen the economic and political position of the Company and about "kind" relations toward the natives. Written at Pavlovsk Harbor, April 19, 1800, In K istorii Rossiisko-Amerikanskoi Kompanii (Sbornik dokumental'nykh materialov). Krasnoiarsk, 1957, pp. 95-106.

*[27]See letter, Baranov to Larionov, from Kad'iak Island, July 24, 1800, in Tikhmenev, II, Appendix, p. 147. Khlebnikov has paraphrased the original, and corrected the grammar.

*[28]Ibid., p. 147.

*[29]Ibid., p. 142.

*30Ibid., p. 150. Khlebnikov fails to mention Kuskov's trouble with the clergy on Kad'iak, who took the plotters' part.

*31This does not appear in Tikhmenev, II, Appendix; perhaps it was omitted in his copy of the document.

*32This does not appear in Tikhmenev.

*33This passage, except for portions mentioned in Notes 31 and 32, is in Tikhmenev, II, Appendix, pp. 154-155.

*34This friction with the Kad'iak natives is recounted by Baranov in his letter to Larionov, March 22, 1801, in Tikhmenev, II, Appendix, p. 164-165. However, Khlebnikov omits mention of Baranov's trouble with the clergy, who sided with the natives.

*35This passage does not appear in the letter mentioned in Note 34, at least not in Tikhmenev's version.

36Ivan Ivanovich Banner was previously on Crown Service in Irkutsk Gubernia and was rural police chief in Zashiversk. Then he left the service and agreed with the Company to take a ship and people to Bering Strait and establish a colony there for trading with the natives. On the way the ship was damaged and put in for a year at the First Kurile Strait. Larionov held the ship at Unalashka, and, considering it unnecessary to have a settlement in the North, sent Banner to Kad'iak where he died in 1816.

*37See Report, Kuskov to Baranov, 1 July 1802, in pp. 106-123.

38See Langsdorf, Voyages and Travels in Various Parts of the World, during the years 1803, 1804, 1805, 1806, and 1807. London, 1814. 2 vols. v. 2, pp. 121-122. D'Wolf "considered it as extremely adventurous in the Russians to think of putting themselves and their ships to so great a hazard."

39See Lisianskii, Travels, Part II in his description of Sitka.

40Those sent were: Andrei Klimovskii, Ivan Chernov and Gerasim Kondakov, who were enrolled in the Navigation School by the Company Administration. They later returned to the colonies. Klimovskii was given command of a vessel, and the others became good mates. Kondakov died in 1820 and Klimovskii in 1831.

*41See Report of Lt. N. A. Khvostov to A. A. Baranov re readiness of vessel Juno for voyage to Kad'iak and other documents regarding preparations for this voyage, October, 1805. <u>K istorii</u>... p. 142-147.

*[42]See letter, Repin, manager of redoubt Konstantin, to Baranov, 24 September 1805. Tikhmenev, II, Appendix, pp. 195-197.

[43]A fanega is equivalent to somewhere between 150 and 160 Russian pounds.

*[44]See letter, Rezanov to Minister of Commerce from Novo-Arkhangel'sk 17 June 1806. Tikhmenev, II, Appendix, pp. 253-283.

[45]Lincoln had been taken into the Company's service in September, 1806 in the capacity of shipbuilder.

[46]The hostages were taken to Kad'iak where, at their own wish they were baptized and given the names Kalistrat and Gedeon. They married there and had children. Later transferred to Sitka, they received a salary and served as interpreters with the Kolosh. Kalistrat died in 1832 but Gedeon survived and is now chief interpreter.

[47]Placing the Aleuts under the supervision of trusted and experienced Russian employees, Baranov, although he could rely on them, nonetheless thought it necessary to make the sanctity of the conditions binding on the seafarers too. Because they were so careful about their profits they would not want to risk sending parties where there might be risk to life and limb, and they therefore always had to be careful, and where necessary to provide strong protection. Here it is evident that Baranov valued his men's lives and did not consider them things, as some strict and selective critics and several foreigners have said who have looked at the matter from a different angle, and motivated by other concepts.

[48]Khristofor Martynovich Benzeman, a Prussian, was taken into Company service from the vessel <u>Peacock</u> of which he was navigator. He commanded Company ships, and has served usefully in the colonies up until the present; he subsequently took out Russian citizenship and, at the suggestion of the Chief Manager, M. N. Murav'ev, he was rewarded with 14th class rank in 1825.

[49]In bartering for powder and guns with the Americans, the Kolosh let no chance slip by of killing them. On March 23, 1803, in Nootka Sound, they wiped out the crew of the <u>Boston</u>, plundered the cargo and burned the ship. Two men escaped and one, John Jewitt, published his account of the incident in Middletown in 1815. See <u>Narrative of the Adventures and Sufferings of John R. Jewitt</u>..., New York, 1815?, and Fairfield, Wash., 1967, with introduction and list of other editions.

[50]See V. M. Golovnin, <u>Sochineniia i perevody</u> (St. P.,
1864, 5 v), Vol. 4 <u>Opisaniia primechatel'nykh korable-</u>
<u>krushenii</u>, including Tarakanov's account of the wreck of
the <u>Sv. Nikolai</u>, pp. 406-428. See also Hector Chevigny,
<u>Russian America. The Great Alaskan Venture, 1741-1867</u>
(New York, 1965), pp. 135-147.

*[51]See agreement of plotters, July 26, 1809, in
<u>K istorii</u>...pp. 166-167.

*[52]See order, Baranov to Hagemeister, on sending ship
<u>Neva</u> to discover new islands between the Kurile Islands
and Kamchatka, November, 1808, <u>K istorii</u>..., pp. 160-166.

*[53]See two letters, Captain-Lieutenant L. A. Hage-
meister to the Directors of the Russian-American Company,
May 1 and June 20, 1809 (paraphrased), describing the
Sandwich Islands, in R. A. Pierce, <u>Russia's Hawaiian</u>
<u>Adventure, 1815-1817</u> (Berkeley, 1965), pp. 37-40.

*[54]For documents concerning Baranov's dealings with
Ebbets, and Astor's proposals, see Kenneth W. Porter,
<u>John Jacob Astor, Businessman</u>, Cambridge, Mass., 1931.
2 vols. I, pp. 428-519, and Ministerstvo Inostrannykh
Del SSSR. <u>Vneshniaia politika Rossii XIX i nachala XX</u>
<u>veka</u>. M., 1967, v. 5, pp. 270-274, and M. 1962, v. ¢,
pp. 711-713.

*[55]Same list of Canton prices, rearranged, appears in
Tikhmenev, I, pp. 180-181.

[56]Ivan Gavrilovich Koch, born in Hamburg, entered
Russian service in a medical capacity in 1769, with the
rank of doctor. He took part in the siege and capture
of Bender in 1770 and the whole Turkish War until the
peace. He was then present in 1777 at the destruction
of the Zaporozh'e Sech' and in the following year in the
Crimea. In 1788 he was promoted to Medical Staff
Officer in the new Irkutsk Namestnichestvo. In 1784 he
was retitled Collegiate Assessor and attached to the
Civil Court in Okhotsk and as Acting Oblast Commandant,
in which he was confirmed and despatched on 15 August
1795. For speedy and accurate execution of these duties
he was made a Chevalier of the Order of St. Vladimir,
4th Class. He was relieved of his duties, and lived
long in Irkutsk while inquiries were conducted into certain shortcomings in his administration of the Wine
Office, at the Provisionary Agency and the wrecks in
1787 and 1788 of the Crown vessels <u>Sv. Pavel</u> and <u>Sv.</u>
<u>Nikolai</u>. In all these inquiries he was vindicated only
in 1802, after which he was for some time Director of
the State textile factory, and because of shortcomings
of the owners, was again under investigation, was vindi-
cated and entered the employ of the Russian-American
Company.

[57]See booklet on the wreck of the <u>Neva</u> by V. N. Berkh, <u>Opisanie neshchastnago korablekrusheniia fregata Rossiisko-Amerikanskoi kompanii Nevy, posledovavshago bliz beregov Novo-Arkhangel'skago Porta</u>. St. P., 1817 (46pp.), and detailed account in V. M. Golovnin's, <u>Sochineniia i perevody</u> (St. P., 1864, 5 v.), IV-V, pp. 444-453.

[58]As the war continued Astor discovered that an English warship had been detailed to capture this colony and hurried, through his connections, to transfer it to the English trading company known at that time as the North West Fur Company, which later (1822) became part of the Hudson Bay Company.

[59]Now that the Columbia belongs to the Hudson Bay Company and comprises the area around Repulse Bay, a permanent line of communication along a well established trail leads to the main settlements in Hudson Bay.

[60]Elliot was picked up by Captain Kotzebue of the brig <u>Rurik</u> and delivered to the Sandwich Islands in 1816. There he took up the rank of State Secretary to His Majesty, King of the Sandwich Islands, Kamehameha. Three Russians were picked up by the <u>Rurik</u> for transfer to St. Petersburg. See the travels of Captain Kotzebue, I, p. 292 ff.

[*61]Khlebnikov omits the fact that Lazarev and Baranov quarelled, and that Lazarev made a hasty departure from Sitka under threat of fire by Baranov.

[62]Kaumualii complained of this to Captain Kotzebue. Otto von Kotzebue, <u>A voyage of discovery into the South Sea and Beering's Straits</u>, 3 v. London, 1821. pp. 302-305.

[*63]See R. A. Pierce, <u>Russia's Hawaiian Adventure, 1815-1817</u>, with list of related works, and N. N. Bolkhovitinov, "Avantiura Doktora Sheffera na Gavaiiakh v 1815-1819," <u>Novaia i noveishaia istoriia</u>, 1972:1, pp. 121-137, based on research in Soviet archives.

[*64]See G. H. Von Langsdorff, <u>Voyages and travels</u>... London, 1814, 2 vols.; II, pp. 32-33.

[*65]See Vancouver, I, pp. 254-257.

[66]See the Appendix to Travels of Captain Golovnin on the sloop <u>Kamchatka</u>.

[67]Letter, Rezanov to Directors of the Russian-American Company, from Novo-Arkhangel'sk, November 6, 1805, in Tikhmenev, II, Appendix, pp. 198-199.

*68_Puteshestviia Davydova_.

69_Puteshestviia Davydova_, Part 2, p. 33.

*70The "partner" was evidently Shelikhov. See letter, Shelikhov and Polevoi to Baranov, from Okhotsk, August 9, 1794, in Tikhmenev, II, Appendix, p. 74; and Letter, Baranov to Shelikhov and Polevoi, from Pavlovsk Harbor, May 20, 1795, _Ibid_., p. 96.

INDEX

KODIAK ISLAND
WITH ITS ENVIRONS 1805
(from Lisianskii)

Shuiak I.

AFOGNAK I.

Co. Settlement

Co. Settlement

Evreshed
(Marmot

North I.

Uganik I.

Elovoi
(Spruce) I.

Pavlovsk (Kodiak)

Lesnoi (Wo

Uganik

Barren I.

West Point

Uiatsk

Uganik

Co. Settlement

Chiniatsk Bay

K
A
D'
I
A
K

Karluk

Igak

Uiak Bay

Igak Bay

S.W.
Point

Kiliuden Bay

Alitak

K

Co.
Settlement

Saltkhidak I.

Three Saints Bay

South Point